British Elizabethan Stamps

BATSFORD STUDIES IN PHILATELY

Advisory Editor: Arthur Blair, FRPSL

David Potter

BRITISH ELIZABETHAN STAMPS

The story of the postage stamps
of the United Kingdom, Guernsey, Jersey and
the Isle of Man, from 1952 to 1970

B. T. Batsford Ltd, London

First published 1971
© David Potter 1971
7134 0381 0

Printed in Great Britain by
Northumberland Press Ltd., Gateshead.
Plates printed and book bound by
Richard Clay (The Chaucer Press) Ltd.,
Bungay, Suffolk

Contents

Illustrations

Preface

More collectors in the British Isles collect Great Britain stamps than any other country. Naturally enough, for they are the easiest to find, at least in the earlier stages. And of these Great Britain collectors, most of them concentrate on the issues of Queen Elizabeth II.

Overseas in the British Commonwealth there is this same keen interest in the stamps of Great Britain. Dealers' advertisements, the local stamp press and society displays, all confirm that Great Britain is a popular country. In the United States there has been a quickening of demand that can be traced back to the awakening of the British Post Office and their revised approach to stamp collectors. Today they actively try to sell modern British stamps and they succeed. The latest area to have taken up Queen Elizabeth British issues is Western Europe, and the Post Office has responded with overseas agencies and translation inserts in their packaged sets. It is for all these groups of collectors that this book is written.

I have aimed to cover every facet of Great Britain stamp collecting, including the sidelines and peripheral groups. There seemed to be no point in copying out long lists that are in any case quite adequately dealt with by the catalogues. Instead this book aims to explain why the stamps were issued, why they changed, why they were withdrawn.

Queen Elizabeth stamps are still being issued as I write, and I trust that this will be the case for many a long year more. But already the listings are lengthening, and the volume increases as the months go by. A natural break is hard to find in a living organism, but at least the change over to decimal currency offers an opportunity to tell the story so far.

I hope that the contents will entertain—for that is in part its purpose. Stamp collecting is a hobby, a pursuit, a relaxation. Nevertheless it is also a subject for study, and to extract full enjoyment it is necessary sometimes to dig in and research. It is hoped that this study will suggest new fields of specialisation.

Significant sections are devoted to stationery, locals and other aspects of Great Britain stamps divorced from the straight-forward adhesive issues. It could be that in some of these groups discoveries will be made in the future. They are certainly neglected at the present time, although no longer completely ignored.

My thanks are due to Arthur Blair, Editor of *Stamp Magazine*, for his helpful comments and suggestions and the painstaking way he read through the manuscript. I trust that there are no errors of fact, but if there are I must take full responsibility.

I duly acknowledge with gratitude the help given by the Post Office for illustrations 40-48, and Link House Publications, for providing some of the illustrations. Most of the material illustrated comes from my own collection.

David Potter
London 1970

1

A New Reign

Stamp collecting started with the penny black. Over the years since 1840 the hobby has become organised. Today there are lists and catalogues, albums and accessories, dealers and magazines.

A new reign brings with it new stamps and new portraits. The beginning of Queen Elizabeth's reign in 1952 was an ideal time to start a collection, but the would-be enthusiast had little to do. For seven or eight years only an occasional commemorative set disturbed the calm. Unless one had access to catalogues or magazines, there was every excuse for thinking that there was but a single set of small size stamps too.

Dedicated collectors knew that changes, albeit unseen, were taking place in the permanent set: watermarks were replaced; phosphor and graphite bands appeared in profusion. But only the enthusiast was excited; the rest did not care. When they did at last take an interest, stocks of these stamps had been dispersed, and were nowhere to be found.

Slowly the now familiar pattern took shape. In 1960 two special sets, and the first large size stamps in two colours, were issued. This was the first sign. The pace quickened. Six, seven, eight or nine new sets of stamps each year. Queues at the post office on the first day. There was no time to be lost. Too slow off the mark, and the stamps were sold out. The die was cast. Great Britain stamps, always popular, went to the top of the charts.

Once committed to a policy of several sets each year, the Post Office looked at the services collectors wanted. They set up the

Philatelic Bureau, provided special posting boxes at the main offices on the day of issue of new stamps, and arranged that all mail posted in them would be carefully postmarked. The time-honoured tradition of calling in at the local office, and sending oneself a set of stamps, underwent a radical change. For years, to ensure a nice clean circular postmark, envelopes were sent by registered or express mail. Now they had to be taken to one of these new philatelic posting boxes. At first scattered thinly, they quickly spread throughout the country. But although the total postage, represented by a complete set, could be several shillings, the prized cancellation reading 'First Day of Issue' was applied only to ordinary mail.

Following a successful pilot scheme, with the Post Office undertaking to service prepared covers for collectors far away from the special boxes, the philatelic machinery moved into gear. Beginning with the Shakespeare set in 1964, special envelopes were printed and used. Stratford-on-Avon must have had one of their heaviest postings ever. So successful was their new policy that today, apart from the stamps themselves, it is possible to purchase blank souvenir envelopes and in most cases presentation packs. Packs were a new departure, containing a set of stamps supported by full details of designs and artists, illustrated in colour and delivered in an attractive wallet. They were not so popular at first. Why pay extra for a set of new stamps, seemed to be the general attitude. With a set such as the Forth Road Bridge, the pack could cost more than the price of the stamps. Ideas changed, and eventually packs became established. Collectors made sure of complete series, and the price of the once despised pack shot up to dizzy heights, to many times its cost a few years earlier.

Breaking into the publication field, the Post Office *Philatelic Bulletin* now enjoys a circulation which commercial stamp magazines can never hope to enjoy. Full-colour illustrations are common, and they are privileged to be able to present the news almost as soon as it happens.

Although the Philatelic Bureau moved to Edinburgh, counters for stamp collectors were opened, and continue to open, around the country. In London, at the Chief Office hard by St Paul's Cathedral, there is inevitably a small queue. Else-where, in the smaller towns, there is often the opportunity to pass the time of day and talk about stamps with the man behind the counter.

The **National Postal Museum**, made possible by private benefaction, has been developed and extended by the Post Office, who have become quick to realise that it is a valuable magnet, especially to visitors from abroad. Tucked away in the same building as the London Philatelic Counter, there are few who fail to call in at both.

In the 1960s stamps multiplied, and the collecting public grew even faster. Magazines became bulkier, dealers' advertisements mushroomed, and the advent of a new colour weekly stamp paper saw a shake-up in all the established periodicals. Colour blossomed forth, if only from the covers, as never before. Such is the power of competition, and the size of the potential market.

Inevitably the money side of collecting came to the fore. It is accepted that over the years the value of stamps will rise. A stamp collector can get perhaps 15 or 20 years of pleasure from his collection and then, if he has been prudent, sell it, covering all expenses and maybe making a small profit. Of course, he would probably have done better to have put all his money on deposit, or invested in a good industrial share, but then he would have missed all the fun.

Suddenly a new force appeared upon the scene. Stamps were bought and sold like so many shares; the speculator had arrived. Buying and selling offers popped up all over the place, stamps were solemnly discussed in the financial columns, usually by those without experience, and the get-rich-quick operators joined in the *mêlée*. Prices seemed to rise each week, at least to the inexperienced. Why bother to work, if all that had to be done was to buy a sheet of each new issue, hide them away for a year, and then sell at a profit? As much as 50 or 100 per cent, income and capital gains tax free, was the lure. It worked for a few. Then, as suddenly as it came, the boom evaporated. Speculators moved on to other fields, leaving chaos and disgruntled holders of stamps. Forced into liquidation at substantial losses, they left the hobby. They were never part of it.

Collecting is not buying sheets from a post office safe, only to tuck them away in another one at home. Collectors look for one of each stamp, or maybe now and then a block of four.

Extra copies above this quota will only find a place when they show some peculiarity or because they tell a story. The collector does not care, within reason, if the price of one set moves up or down. He looks at the lot, as a whole. Even as the bottom dropped out of the market in some special issues, other Queen Elizabeth stamps became popular and pricier. The definitives, now studied for their watermarks, were wanted. Phosphor-lined varieties were in demand. Every single year the collector of all modern Great Britain stamps has seen some section go forward, more than compensating for setbacks in other areas.

This is not for the speculator. Collections, unlike sheets, are not to be found for the asking. They have to be painstakingly built up, and they grow with the enthusiasm of the owner. Branching out in many directions, reflecting personal whims and fancies, a good collection expresses the spirit of its owner. A quiet relaxing hobby, with a modicum of reward—that is philately. What is more natural than to collect and specialise in the current issues, and the earlier ones, of the first stamp nation in the world—Great Britain?

2

The Wilding Definitives

'Her Most Excellent Majesty Elizabeth the Second, by the Grace of God, of the United Kingdom of Great Britain and Northern Ireland, and of Her other Realms and Territories Queen, Head of the Commonwealth.' So runs the style and title of Queen Elizabeth II, who succeeded to the throne on 6 February 1952.

The first Elizabethan designs were unveiled, and the stamps released, on 5 December 1952, just ten months after the accession. In that short space of time 74 designs were submitted for consideration. The initial choice fell to an advisory panel, with representatives from the Council of Industrial Design, the Royal Fine Arts Commission and the Arts Council of Great Britain, the College of Arms. Philately was represented by Sir John Wilson, Bt, then Keeper of the Royal Philatelic Collection. With their help, the Postmaster-General made a selection, which was forwarded to the Queen, who naturally took the final decision.

For the central feature a photograph of the Queen by Dorothy Wilding Portraits Limited was chosen. Unusual at that time, so far as Great Britain stamps were concerned, it showed a three-quarter portrait, in marked contrast to the side view of its immediate predecessors. The official reasoning was that a photograph was ideally suited to the photogravure process of printing, although collectors' reception of the stamps themselves was rather mixed.

Miss Enid Marx, RDI, FSIA, designed the $1\frac{1}{2}$d value. Well-known for her book illustrations, this was her first postage stamp design. She surrounded the portrait by a circlet of the national emblems, rose, thistle, shamrock and daffodil.

M. C. Farrar-Bell created the 2½d. A typographer-designer and painter of inn signs, noted for his stained-glass work, examples of his design and restoration techniques are to be found at Bath Abbey and Exeter Cathedral. He framed the head of the 2½d with an ornamental oval, placing the four heraldic flowers in the lower left corner, neatly balancing the value tablet at the right. A symmetrical effect was achieved by the unusual use, in the 1950s, of the sovereign's monogram, with the letters ER in the upper corners.

A further instalment of this definitive, or permanent stamp issue, arrived on 6 July 1953, when the 5d, 8d and 1s, each different, completed the range of designs. G. Knipe, an artist-designer on the staff of Harrison and Sons, the printers, prepared the 5d, 6d and 7d. Miss Adshead designed the 8d, 9d, 10d and 11d, while Edmund Dulac was responsible for the 1s, 1s 3d, and 1s 6d.

The members of this trio were established designers, with previous Great Britain stamps to their credit. Conversely the first two artists were newcomers to the field.

Later the 1½d design was used for four values ½d, 1d, 1½d and 2d, and the 2½d shared its composition with 3d and 4d, to be joined some years later by the 4½d.

The common features in all definitive stamps are the Dorothy Wilding Portrait of the Queen, the words 'Postage' and 'Revenue', and the heraldic flowers. The designers were faced with the problem of arranging these essentials, adding any touches they considered necessary. Probably the element that posed the greatest difficulty was the positioning of the value. Solutions varied from rendering it in words by Knipe, pushing it into the only bit of spare space by Miss Adshead, or placing it neatly at the foot of the stamp, by Dulac. The value, an essential part of a postage stamp, is always a headache, especially if more than one denomination shares the same design. Numbers and combinations of numbers take up differing amounts of space.

This issue was completed in four further instalments of three: ½d, 1d, 2d on 31 August 1953; 4d, 1s 3d, 1s 6d, on 2 November; 3d, 6d, 7d on 18 January; and 9d, 10d, 11d on 8 February 1954. Fourteen months for 17 different stamps was a remarkable

I. THE WILDING DEFINITIVES

2. THE FIRST ELIZABETHAN COMMEMORATIVES
The four Coronation designs and two of the Scout Jubilee Jamboree
stamps

achievement, especially at that time with such heavy demands on printers' capacity. Two of these denominations, 1s 3d and 1s 6d, were quite new in Great Britain. They were introduced to cover the half-ounce basic airmail letter rates. These were, at that time, 1s 3d to Zone B (the Americas, most of Africa, and parts of Asia), and 1s 6d to Zone C (the Far East, Australasia and Oceania).

All the stamps were printed on a paper with a new watermark. Over the years the postal authorities had been preoccupied with security, and it had become the custom to prepare special paper with a distinctive device. It was the custom to use the monarch's personal monogram, or an adaption of it. So, in addition to the new designs, new paper was also introduced. Now known as the Tudor watermark, the Imperial Crown surmounts the Royal Cypher, E 2 R, positioned in a multiple, staggered arrangement, covering the complete sheet. It was announced in 1954, soon after the complete set had been issued, that: 'In compliance with the wish of Her Majesty the Queen, the crown bits in the watermark of current British stamps are to be replaced with new ones showing St Edward's Crown.'

Both these crowns are included in the 1s 6d Coronation commemorative design. From an heraldic point of view, the Tudor crown is in an imperial style. In the St Edward's Crown the arch dips towards the centre, the accepted style for a kingdom.

Advance warning of the replacement of individual values was not forthcoming, and the change was gradual. First noted on stamps from booklets in August 1955, it took a full year to complete the changeover. A further variation in 1958 retained the crown, but removed the cypher, presenting an all-over crown watermark. Once again the stamps appeared gradually, as the earlier printings on St Edward's watermarked paper were exhausted.

The reasons for this last change are shrouded in mystery. A number of theories have been advanced, from the technical supposition that sharp corners of the letters were unacceptable, to the feeling that it was a political compromise, in deference to Scottish nationalism. It is doubtful if the true story will ever be known.

In 1962 there was an official announcement stating that in future all stamps were to be printed on an optically white paper, in order to improve the quality and appearance of the issue. A comparison between old and new papers is readily made with mint marginal blocks, but it is more difficult with single copies, used or unused. There is a pronounced tendency, on many denominations, for the colour to suffuse onto the narrow margin of the stamps. In addition, positive identification is confused by a series of unannounced trials with different types of paper. These are partly distinguishable by experts, but without official assistance progress has been slow. Paper differences are also discernible under an ultra-violet lamp, and here again there is a wide spectrum of reactions. Optical whitener is used in the making of the paper, and variations in raw materials, and even the water used in manufacture, can also present different optical readings.

One interesting experiment was officially noted. To assist research into paper stretching, which had caused considerable discrepancies in the number of sheets obtained from one reel, a slightly heavier quality than normal was used. A special watermark, in the form of a sideways T, appeared two or four times at the edges of the sheet, in addition to the normal crowns. 48,000 sheets of 3d stamps were printed, but the results were inconclusive, and the test was not repeated.

All watermarks are best observed by placing the stamp, design side face downwards, on a dark surface. The watermark will stand out in darker relief. With the last multiple crown watermark it can be quite hard to distinguish. In these cases some solvents such as lighter fuel may help, but it should be used with caution, in small quantities. It will not damage the design or the gum, but it will adversely affect phosphor bands.

For a set with a life of over 16 years there are remarkably few variations in colours, or in denominations. The colours for the lower values were in the same deep tones used in 1937. These had been weakened, almost certainly as a war economy measure, although some sources suggest that it was an anti-forgery precaution. Rumours from German sources indicated that the Axis powers were experimenting with the production of British stamps as part of an assault upon the economy. The colour of the 2d stamp had been changed in 1951 from orange to brown to conform with Universal Postal Union regulations. This value was widely used on stamped receipts, and the deep tone of brown made the deciphering of signatures rather difficult. After some three years of discussion, the colour was changed to lighter brown in October 1956, during the currency of the St Edward's watermark.

An announced change of colour for the 6d, from reddish purple to deep claret, took place in May 1958, after the original ink proved difficult to obtain.

Lastly, on 17 May 1965 the basic inland letter rate was raised to 4d, from 3d. Overnight, the demand for 4d stamps increased phenomenally, and it was considered that the light pastel shade would be difficult to maintain throughout large printing runs. So a deeper, darker shade of blue appeared on 28 April 1965, anticipating the demand.

Other shades of most values exist. These are due simply to the problems associated with matching colours over a long period. They are listed in the specialist catalogues, and are collected by dedicated enthusiasts. To be noteworthy they must be plainly distinguishable to the eye, and show some consistency.

It was an earlier postage rise on 1 October 1957 that raised the charge for letters between one and two ounces from $2\frac{1}{2}$d to $4\frac{1}{2}$d. Large business mailings frequently attracted this rate, and it could only be satisfied by either using two dissimilar denominations, or a strip of three $1\frac{1}{2}$d stamps. Neither course was very helpful when a large number of packets was involved. This inconvenience came to an end 16 months later on 9 February 1959, when a $4\frac{1}{2}$d value was added to the series. An interesting reflection on the times, the last $4\frac{1}{2}$d had been sold in Queen Victoria's time, when it covered the parcel postage between one and two pounds.

It was decided not to reprint the 11d stamp, and the St Edward's watermarked version was sold to exhaustion. Practically the only use for this odd denomination was as a make-up value on postal orders. It lingered on for a short time, as part of the set sold in prototype presentation packs.

One further change of specialist interest involves two types of the $2\frac{1}{2}$d. In the first stages of printing a multipositive is prepared, from which the printing cylinders are made. Soon after the first release of this value in sheet form it was considered that a slight improvement could be made to the lines of the Queen's diadem. This was done, and a new multipositive was made and put on one side until new cylinders were needed. It was in fact used to make up a booklet cylinder, and it was from the Post Office books that the new type was first recognised. Two types of 2½d remained in use throughout the life of this stamp, for at peak periods old cylinders were pressed into service to meet demand. Two types of 2½d exist on all three watermarks.

Booklet stamps, because of their special make-up, include inverted or sideways watermark varieties. Certain stamps in rolls are also known with sideways watermark.

From 1957 stamps began to appear with marks on the face or reverse. They were heralds of an automated age. Transportation of mail accounts for but a small fraction of total overheads. On average some 40 per cent of expenditure is attributable to handling; the more times a single letter needs sorting, the greater the final cost. In the twentieth century there is a continued history of inflation, and wages rise to combat it. Accordingly the Post Office investigated, using modern work study techniques, all the operations involved in handling a letter, from the time it was collected from a postbox until it was delivered to the addressee.

One salient factor emerged. Facing the letters, that is putting them into a position to receive a cancellation, took up a significant portion of the handling time. If this stage could be eliminated, then substantial savings would result. The Post Office Engineering Department carried out a number of experiments designed to make this process fully automated. In the early stages they constructed an Automatic Letter Facer, nick-named ALF. In the prototype an electrical sensor located stamps which had been specially treated with graphite lines. These lines were made up from colloidal graphite 'Dag 1928' developed by Acheson Colloids Limited of Plymouth. It was printed as a continuous electrically conducting line, and the first stamps so treated were placed on sale at all post offices within a 30-mile radius of Southampton Head Office, on 19 November 1957.

One month later, on 19 December 1957, in a blaze of nation-wide publicity the Postmaster-General switched on the machine, and the automatic facing and cancellation of letters commenced. Six values were modified, the low denominations from ½d to 3d on St Edward's watermark paper. At that time the printed postage rate was 2d, and this value was processed with one vertical line. All the other stamps had two lines. In peak periods envelopes bearing only a 2d stamp would be stockpiled by the machine, after postmarking, for attention later on. Fully paid 3d mail received priority treatment. Awkward packages, and those prepaid by means of conventional postage stamps, were also diverted, to be dealt with by hand. These experimental stamps were not expected to sell in large numbers, and they were printed from single cylinder sheets, compared with the normal twin sheets cylinders normally used. As it transpired, this was not a wise decision, for the 3d alone sold over 90 million copies.

A second issue, one year later, was made on crown watermark paper, 2d, 2½d and 3d issued in sheets, and two new treated denominations 4d and 4½d. Booklets containing ½d, 1d, 1½d, 2½d and 3d stamps, and coils of the ½d, 1d, 2d and 3d were also released. The comparative scarcity of the 1½d is explained by its issue only in booklet form. Less than two million were printed, half with watermark inverted. Even the other low values, ½d and 1d with all-over crown watermark, and the 2½d with watermark inverted are scarce.

Towards the end of 1959, the experiments took a new turn. Electrical sensing was dropped and an optical system was introduced. Since the graphite treated stamps would no longer be needed, and in preparation for the second stage of the trials, some 20,000 sheets of 2d and 3d, and 3,000 sheets of the other six values were overprinted with phosphor bands by typography. A number of sheets were spoilt in the process, accounting for the discrepancy between numbers ordered and issued. By error, a small quantity of the old St Edward's crown 2d was included; otherwise the three low values were on the original paper and the 2d to 4½d were on all-over crown paper.

These stamps were issued on 18 November 1959, and served the dual purpose of reacting to either form of scanning during the change-over period. Disregarding the 2d error, only 490,560 sets were issued, and most of these were used up in the normal way.

Phosphor bands are practically invisible in normal light. If the stamp is held a foot or so in front of the eyes, and the light is allowed to fall obliquely onto the surface, they will be easily seen. They appear as matt, misty lines and run vertically over the face of the stamp. They can also be observed under an ultra-violet lamp, emitting in the 2000-4000 Angstrom Units range.

Once the modifications had been completed, the graphite stamps had outlived their usefulness. Remaining stocks of sheet stamps were issued indiscriminately outside the Southampton area, and so too were the booklets. Some paper were left over, and a special printing was made. Booklet paper was used for a 1d printing, which was then split into Post Office rolls. Because the layout of the lines for booklets does not coincide with their placing for sheets, a number of misplaced line varieties were issued, and many of these found their way into philatelic hands. They are hardly errors, for the printing was made deliberately, but they do form an interesting group. Instead of two lines, one on each side of the stamp, successive displacements produce one line, two lines, to the right or left, and even three line variations.

Next stage in the experiment required phosphor only treated stamps. They were originally confined to the Southampton Post Office area only, and they were not despatched to the surrounding countryside like their predecessors. First to appear on 22 June 1960 were the $\frac{1}{2}$d to 4d, 6d and 1s 3d. Unlike the provisional phosphor-graphite stamps, the lines were this time applied by photogravure. This phosphor material, ρ-hydroxy diphenyl, is commercially known as Lettalite B.1, and is referred to as green phosphor by collectors. This is the colour of the phosphorescence when it reacts to ultra-violet light in the 2000-3000 Angstrom Units range.

The optical modifications proved acceptable, and a purpose-built facing machine was manufactured and installed in Southampton on 1 August 1961. In preparation for the adoption of automatic facing, the first treated stamps that could reasonably be called permanent, rather than experimental, appeared on 5 June 1961. A similar range to the 1960 issue, with the addition of a 4$\frac{1}{2}$d, was treated, but the phosphor substance was changed to carbasone sulphonic acid. Com-mercially known as Lettalite B.2, it is called blue phosphor by the Post Office and collectors. It reacts to 2000-4000 Angstrom Units light, with a bluish colour, and was chosen because it had a better response and lower solubility in water.

These stamps enjoyed a life of four years, and they were placed on sale in other parts of the country, as new machines were installed. Automatic facing became the normal method in south-east London from October 1962, then at Liverpool and Glasgow, to be followed by Norwich in November 1965.

Norwich had been the guinea-pig area for another of the automation experiments, postal coding. Letters were sorted there by phosphor-coded marks, and the blue phosphor stamps would have interfered with this process. So a third type of phosphor was introduced. Nevertheless, during the blue phosphor life there had been two changes in the printed postage rates, and so successively both 2½d and 3d were treated with one phosphor line, and in compensation the 2d and then the 2½d reverted to two lines. Sideways and inverted watermark varieties came from booklets. Lettalite B.3 or tere-phthalic acid became known as violet phosphor. Like its green predecessor it reacted to the 2000-3000 Angstrom Units ultra-violet light range. The phosphor bands so far produced were 8mm wide, except for the stamps indicating the printed postage rate, which had a single 4mm line at the left. Booklet stamps in some cases had the single line applied at either the left or right. Eight stamps were treated, and placed on sale from 13 August 1965.

When west London installed a machine in August 1967, the entire London Postal Region went over to phosphor-lined stamps, and by 1967 the Post Office conceded that the extra cost of treatment was more than offset by the possible savings at the Supplies Depot, where two separate stocks were maintained. Accordingly it became the policy to have all new printings made with phosphor lines. About this time too, the double lined stamps had the band thickness increased to 9.5mm, and the single lines were centrally placed. These minor alterations were presumably to enable ALF to distinguish between the two types of mail, even if there was a gross line displacement on the stamps.

The odd halfpenny values, ½d, 1½d, 2½d, and 4½d, did not receive these extra-wide lines, probably because stocks of earlier printings remained. There was little call for these denominations, and in some places they were not even stocked. In fact the 2½d and 4½d did not receive the violet lines at all, blue phosphor remaining in use right up to their date of withdrawal. All the other current definitive stamps appeared with these final type of phosphor lines, over a period of months.

A one-day strike, and overtime ban by postal staff in the spring of 1965, led to a severe shortage of 1d and 4d stamps. Bisected 2d and 8d values are known, but they were never officially authorised. Those that were so used, and escaped postage due, did so by courtesy rather than by right. Such bisected stamps are well worth a place in a collection, but they must be on cover, with the postmark overlapping both stamp and paper, tying it to the piece. Prepayment in cash was the accepted method of dealing with the shortage, and most of such covers are indistinguishable from the normal prepayment facilities available at all main offices.

As the Machin Head permanent series was introduced, post offices continued to use up their stocks, and for a time continued to receive residual supplies. By the end of 1968 they had virtually disappeared from the counters, although they continued to be sold at the Philatelic Bureau and its branches up to 27 February 1970, when they at last became obsolete. Like all stamps issued from 1911, they remained valid for postage. At the end, only four ordinary and 14 phosphor-treated stamps remained on sale. All the remaining values were exhausted.

Some of this issue, in the earlier watermarks, exist overprinted and in some cases surcharged. Although not *British* Elizabethan stamps, they are referred to here for completeness. British post offices selling overprinted stamps with values in annas and rupees, or naye paise, were maintained in the Persian Gulf. These stamps were on sale in Bahrain until 1960, Kuwait until 1959, Muscat, Dubai and other agencies until 1964 and Qatar until 1963. Those without the name of a country are to be found in the catalogues under Muscat, but although intended for specific areas were on sale generally at all British postal agencies in the Persian Gulf. They were not valid for postage in Great Britain.

There was a different situation at the British post offices at Tetuan, in northern Morocco, and at Tangier in the International Zone. These stamps were overprinted, but not surcharged, with the exception of four stamps, expressed in centimos, sold in the Spanish Zone of Morocco. All these North African issues, with values still expressed in shillings and pence, were allowed by favour to be used on mail in Great Britain.

A strange situation indeed. These stamps were on sale outside the sterling area, and could not be purchased direct. But they were available, by post, in sheets from the British Post Office in London. Once purchased, they could be freely used in Great Britain for any postal function, although this regulation was not generally known outside philatelic circles. They are often encountered with British postmarks, for they were popular with stamp dealers who would use them to give their customers philatelic franking at a time when there were few commemoratives to be found.

Whatever the standard of collection, or depth of knowledge, one salient fact remains: the watermarks, overprints and experimental markings make up a definitive set, full of interest, and well worth studying. It is not easy to complete, but it does provide a not unattainable challenge.

3

The Commemoratives

Look for the cause of the upsurge in collecting interest. Explain the influx into the ranks of stamp collectors. Invariably it is the steady stream of brightly coloured commemorative and special issues from the Post Office. Their regular appearance on mail is a continuous advertisement for the hobby. It is a familiar sight, on the first day of release of a new set, to see a constant queue of ready buyers. Just purchasing a few sets to put on one side, either for their own enjoyment, or for the future collections of their children.

It was not always so. At the beginning of the reign the stamp policy for new sets was to prepare issues marking events of national, international or Post Office significance. Naturally enough the Coronation fell into this category. Coronation Day was a public holiday, with most of the population engaged in lining the route, or watching with more comfort and wider coverage as the splendour unfolded on television. So the following day, 3 June 1953, was chosen for the day of release of four commemorative stamps.

So few were the opportunities to prepare new stamps that the designers seemed to try and fit everything within a small canvas. Six items of regalia were placed into a space 40 by 23mm, and in addition the Dorothy Wilding portrait of the Queen was arranged with sprays, denomination and inscription, to provide a pleasing effect by Mr Edgar Fuller. He achieved the impossible on the $2\frac{1}{2}$d, the most commonly seen denomination. (His other work at that time included the reverse of the 5s piece.) Mr Michael Goaman had basically the same idea for the

4d, but was stumped when positioning the crown, which sitting above the diadem head looks incongruous.

Edmund Dulac, designer of the King George VI Coronation stamp, used an entirely different approach, and instead of the standard portrait chose a symbolic robed and crowned full face head and shoulders. This centrepiece is backed by a Tudor tapestry background, and although the area is fully used on the 1s 3d, it all falls together quite naturally. Simpler and straightforward is the top value, 1s 6d. The only one of the four to bear the date, it also utilises the Wilding portrait. A long and popular sale followed the print order of over 400 million 2½d, and 32 million in all of the higher values.

In 1956 the policy for new issues was relaxed to the extent that in future at least one special series would appear each year. The rule was restated as 'current events of outstanding national and international importance, and historic dates of Royal or postal significance'.

It was fortunate for the Boy Scout movement, celebrating its fiftieth anniversary with an International Jamboree at Sutton Park, Sutton Coldfield, Warwickshire, that this reappraisal had been completed. On 1 August 1957 they were honoured with three stamps, featuring scout badges and supporting symbolic elements. In place of the Tudor watermark paper used for the Coronation, these were printed on contemporary St Edward's crown sheets.

Also as part of the new appraisement by the Post Office, they offered a simple first day cover service. To streamline handling and preparation, an experimental machine had been developed. This automatically affixed the stamps, from continuous rolls of 4,800, to the envelopes. From 480 to 487 such rolls were prepared for each denomination, and apparently the project fell far short of expectations. The total used, including direct sales to collectors, was a mere 23 rolls of 2½d, 21 of 4d and 20 of the 1s 3d. Ten rolls of each value were repackaged in smaller coils, but even these were ignored, only 49, 37 and 33 respectively finding purchasers.

In September 1957 the 46th Interparliamentary Union Congress was held in London, and one small-size stamp appeared. Apart from its small size, unique in commemorative issues of the present reign, it would seem that the authorities had resisted such an emission until the last minute, and then with ill grace capitulated. How else can the poor adaption from the then current definitives and the choice of the 4d foreign postage rates be explained. Outside the stamp collecting fraternity few knew that such an issue existed. Mint copies were ignored, used copies overlooked, and in due time the stamps rose quickly in value, to 15 times its face value in 1970.

Cardiff was the host to the British Commonwealth and Empire Games, held in Cardiff from 18 July 1958, and this was the subject of the next special series. Again there were three denominations, 3d for inland letters, 6d for foreign surface mail, and 1s 3d for certain airmail letters. They enjoyed a prolonged sale, were still on sale in September, and over 320 million of the lowest value alone were printed.

The tercentenary of the General Letter Office, commemorated by two stamps on 7 July 1960, marked the end of one decade, and the beginning of the next. They were the last commemoratives to appear, as a complete monochrome set, and the first to use multiple crown paper. The first vertical format double-size stamp was issued, and the break-away from tradition was a harbinger of changes to come. This was the initial timid experimental step.

So to the excitement of two colours, for a lack-lustre event— the first anniversary of the Conference of European Postal and Telecommunications Administrations. Most of the general public never saw them; the denominations had limited domestic use. The Post Office adapted the design adopted by other countries honouring the conference, with the Queen's head in place of the territorial name.

Policy was again eased in 1961, by aiming at two special sets in a year instead of one. In the second half of that year there were in fact three such series. A notable Post Office anniversary, the Post Office Savings Bank, attracted three values. Two, the $2\frac{1}{2}$d and 3d, for inland cards and letters, assured a wide distribution for this public relations exercise. These lower values were printed on two different presses producing easily distinguishable variations, now called the Timson and Thrissell printings after the machines that made them. To separate and classify the printings, the portrait is the best guide. On the $2\frac{1}{2}$d, the background is a deep black, and the Queen's face quite a deep grey

3. EARLY COMMEMORATIVE STATIONERY
Airletter designed to celebrate the Coronation. Adhesive small size
Parliamentary Commemorative and the overprinted new design
for airletters

4. SCOUT JAMBOREE COIL LEADERS
This was the only Elizabethan Commemorative produced in coil
form, used in conjunction with the automatic first day cover
servicing equipment

from the Timson printing. By contrast, the Thrissell version background is slightly paler and the portrait considerably lighter. The Timson 3d portrait is clear and well-defined, bright with distinct tones. On the other hand a dull featureless face was produced by the Thrissell machine.

A second Europa set followed in September, and the Post Office was quick to make the point that this was not to be an annual affair. 1961 was an exception, with Great Britain as the hosts to the conference at Torquay. The year concluded with two stamps for the Seventh Parliamentary Conference, the first stamps to be produced from a finer screen of 250 lines to the inch. All earlier photogravure issues had been printed to a 200-line standard.

Eight stamps in the year, and eight different denominations. At the time the aim was to avoid duplication. This policy succeeded, but only just, and some odd postal uses were conjured up: $2\frac{1}{2}$d postcards, 3d letters, and 1s 6d airmail for the bank issue, 6d foreign and 1s 3d airmail rates for the Parliamentary pair, left little in reserve for the final set. So the Europa trio covered 2d printed paper, 4d second printed paper band, and 10d second stage foreign mail.

In contrast there was just one special series in 1962. On 14 November, as publicity for the National Productivity Year launched by HRH the Duke of Edinburgh, three stamps by one designer, David Gentleman, maintained uniformity, although symbolism remained supreme. These were the first commemoratives with phosphor bands. Their sale was confined to Southampton, Liverpool and London SE1, the only offices with automatic equipment. The rest of the country received untreated stamps.

One set in 1962, but six series in 1963, 12 stamps in all. Freedom from Hunger, the Paris Postal Conference and National Nature Week followed in quick succession, and again each denomination was different. The unusual $4\frac{1}{2}$d value pre-paid inland letters weighing between one and two ounces. The first two of these issues, in common with the National Productivity Year set, were printed on paper with watermark inverted. An official explanation stated that the reels had cracked after coating, and it was feared that they would suffer breaks during the printing run. To reduce the risk they remained wound in reverse, so that inverted watermarks for these three sets are normal, and only exist so.

International Lifeboat Conference, Red Cross Centenary, and the Compac single completed the year's programme, and although the lower denominations were assorted, no less than three 1s 6d stamps exist. Owing to their high value, few were aware of their existence, and this is especially so for the Compac stamp. Commemorating the opening of the Commonwealth Pacific Cable, it shared the essential elements of the design used also by Australia and New Zealand.

Five stamps, including a 2s 6d, were placed on sale from 23 April 1964, officially in commemoration of the Shakespeare Festival. It is no coincidence that the first day of issue was also the bard's 400th birthday. Two printers shared the contract, Harrison and Sons, and Bradbury, Wilkinson. David Gentleman was again the designer of the photogravure stamps, but different artists, C. and R. Ironside, completed the series. This different-size stamp, printed by recess, interrupted the unity of the set. 2s 6d met few postage rates, except for occasional items between half and one ounce sent by airmail, or an inland four-pound parcel, but it was nevertheless in great demand. In part this was due to the advance announcement of the limited printing figures. This caused some investment buying, and later printings to replenish stocks came in a different shade. Add to this the excitement of a very few copies found in a jet black colour, compared to the more normal violet and brownish blacks, and the four million sales are seen in perspective. It it generally accepted that the jet black stamps were proof sheets, or colour trials, that inadvertently were mixed up with the normal printing.

1964 continued with two more four-value sets for the 20th International Geographical Congress and the 10th International Botanical Congress. The year concluded with a pair for the opening of the Forth Road Bridge. The 8d Geographical with phosphor lines enjoyed a record low printing of under half a million. Only some airmail postcards attracted this odd 8d fee, and the demand was small, for the area of use was still confined to four towns. Glasgow had joined in from April 1963.

What a year 1965 was, both for the collector and for the Post Office! Anthony Wedgwood Benn, the Postmaster-General announced that a wider, less restrictive basis would be adopted forthwith for new special issues. Speaking on 15 December 1964 he stated that stamps would be prepared to celebrate events of national and international importance, commemorate important anniversaries, reflect the British contribution to world affairs and extend public patronage to the arts by encouraging the development of miniscule art.

The decision made, they went to it with a vengeance. Nine special commemorative sets appeared, but not always when they were planned. There was a labour dispute within the Post Office, and an overtime ban by the Supplies Department personnel impeded deliveries. It was intended that the centenary of the International Telecommunications Union pair would be the first to appear, but in the event they were postponed six months, from 17 May to 15 November. First on the scene were the Winston Churchill memorial pair, scheduled for Commonwealth Day, 24 May, but delayed to 8 July.

Two machines were used for the 4d value. A new rotary Rembrandt machine was used at first, but as the printing proceeded a progressively poorer impression of the design appeared. Harrisons switched to the Timson machine, used for some of the Post Office Savings Bank sheets. There was some excitement in the popular press, as case after case of a broken white line was reported. In fact the line was printed in two operations, as part of the bicolour production, and the very accurate registration required was not forthcoming. This is not uncommon in multicolour printing, but it is only apparent when part of the design runs on through two or more colours. Otherwise it usually passes unnoticed. On this issue it cuts Churchill's shoulder, to make a panel for the denomination.

Nearly six weeks later than planned, on 18 July, the 700th anniversary of Simon de Montfort's Parliament pair was placed on sale. Another first, the 2s 6d was three times rather than twice the normal length, showing a panorama of the riverside in 1267. Unlike the lower denominations, the 2s 6d is never treated with phosphor bands. In contrast to other Elizabethan high values, this was the only one to be produced by photogravure.

Centennials for the Salvation Army, and Joseph Lister's antiseptic surgery both merited a pair of stamps, and both were delayed. Lister appeared at the same time as the Commonwealth Arts festival 6d and 1s 6d, so two sets shared a single day of release.

Battle of Britain 1940 was remembered by another skirmish 25 years later. This was the struggle of collectors trying to fit the complete set onto an envelope, and the encounter with the public, some of whom did not see eye to eye with the designs. At that time many commercial firms were supplying printed first-day envelopes, to be used by their purchasers on the day of issue. Naturally plans and printing were completed well in advance to effect distribution. Suddenly, in August, it was announced that the already publicised issue was to break new ground. Instead of the expected single 4d value there were to be six, printed se-tenant in the sheet, in a block arrangement, two rows of three stamps. Uproar ensued, for the small envelopes were now useless, unable to accommodate this extra-size block. With eight stamps to the set, this was the largest number to date, contrasting with the familiar pairs.

To add to the hubbub, a campaign was mounted against the use of either swastika or Iron Cross in the designs. Exchanges in Parliament, and in the newspapers, did not deter the authorities. Instead they explained that the public could refuse to accept any particular design; what the counter-staff thought is not recorded. Despite the fuss, only 337 swastika and 323 Iron Cross stamps were returned for destruction.

London's new landmark, the Post Office Tower, also got its own pair of stamps, and again a vertical design was incorporated, almost a necessity with a building 600 feet high! Phosphor lines were applied to this format for the first time; they are in some cases extraordinarily difficult to see with the naked eye. Unsold stocks were reserved for sale from the public viewing platform of the Tower itself, and so remained in use for a long period. This was the first set to include the artist's name, and the name of the printers.

Two more pairs completed the marathon year. United Nations twentieth anniversary and the Telecommunications issue, both postponed from earlier. The ITU pair are noteworthy for the very small number printed with phosphor bands. Only 600,000 were issued of each value, and the 1s 6d quickly sold out, with the corresponding steep rises in the price asked by dealers. Strangely the lower 9d denomination with exactly the

5. COMMEMORATIVES IN THE EARLY 1960s
National Nature Week, including the unusual 4½d denomination.
Lifeboat Conference designs, with their striking white background.
Botanical Congress, showing flowers, an early thematic subject.
United Nations, in contrast, with the symbolic design

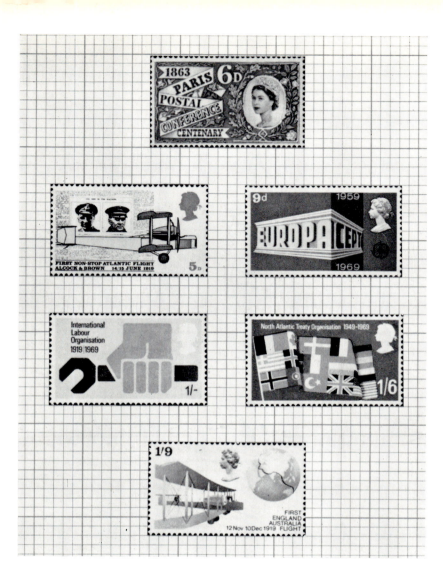

6. ANNIVERSARIES

1963 Paris Conference 6d, one of the few single stamp issues.
Solution 1969 style, with five separate commemorations each with
their own stamp, issued on one day

same printing figure remained on sale for a further six months at the Philatelic Bureau, and at the special philatelic counters, until withdrawn in the normal way.

1966, and the pace quickened. Nine sets, but 30 stamps, breaking the record for special issues, with more excitement and fresh innovations. First of the year was a pair of Robert Burns, whose 200th birthday had passed unnoticed. In the dark ages of official policy, despite pressure from Scottish interests, the veto on such frivolities was absolute. Now the 207th anniversary of the poet's birth, was the date chosen for belated commemoration, as a counterweight to the attention given to England's William Shakespeare.

Westminster Abbey collected a 3d and 2s 6d, the higher value finely produced by recess, to be followed by the first special issue in no way linked to any event or anniversary. Hailed as a bold new departure, four landscape pictorials were released, and received with disappointment by the collecting community. Pictorials from around the world are there in plenty, to be compared, and to set a standard. As an idea it was fine, but with poor designs it failed to make the grade. A political balance was achieved with typical views from the four countries of the United Kingdom. Symbolic, rather than photographic pictures, they can be summed up by the 4d, simply labelled Sussex, and it could be anywhere! Only Wales with its 1s 3d Harlech Castle comes near to capturing the spirit of the countryside. Another innovation, first applied to this series, was the cameo portrait adopted by David Gentleman from the coinage head.

With such special series there is no need to link the date of issue to a specific day in the calendar. Originally intended for 26 April, they were delayed to 2 May, to ease production and distribution difficulties.

England, as hosts to the World Cup, welcomed 15 other teams for the final stages of the competition to win the coveted gold cup. The trophy was on show that year at Britain's National Stamp Exhibition, Stampex, and it was stolen during the course of the show. Happily recovered, the exhibition collected unparalleled publicity, although ruefully it was suggested that this could well have been one piece of news they could have done without. Three stamps were printed, and as soon as the cup was well and truly won by England, the Post Office put into motion the necessary steps for an extra issue.

Perhaps at that time they wished that they had not bothered. Everything that could be calculated to upset a public relations exercise seemed to happen at once. The fatal mistake was to announce in advance that only 12 million were to be printed. Quick calculations by astute businessmen showed that £100,000 was enough to buy up the issue outright. In other words, the stamp must be scarce, and a sheet or two was a sure-fire investment.

Long before the day of release the Philatelic Bureau announced that they could accept no more orders. On the day there were scenes at the all-night post office in Trafalgar Square. From the hour of midnight, the crowd jostled and swayed to purchase the magic stamps, the easy road to a fortune. By 12.25 a.m. over 100,000 stamps, the entire supply to this office, had been exhausted. At local offices, where collectors were used to buying five or six sheets for postage, the entire allocation was perhaps two sheets, or even less. For those with the time and patience, there was the chance to scour the suburbs and countryside, snapping up any unsold specimens.

Meanwhile, the speculators were in full cry, the daily press had taken up the story, and sheets were quoted on the Stock Exchange, albeit unofficially, until they put a ban on such transactions. Retail prices shot up, 3s 6d on the day of issue in Central London, and only available from a stamp shop. Few were used on letters, for here was a commodity worth its weight in precious metal. Or so they thought. Advertisements appeared in the personal columns, in a tone normally reserved for Centre Court seats at Wimbledon, or a Gala performance at Covent Garden. But like all bubbles it had to burst; eventually the slump set in. Buying at 6d, selling at 9d was the market rate three years later. Twelve million stamps, most retained unused, was too much, even for the vast army of British collectors. Strangely one result of the frenzy is that nicely used, contemporary dated copies are difficult to find, although some of them were used commercially when sold from small post offices with no collecting clientele.

Overshadowed by the intoxication of World Cup fever a block of four stamps se-tenant, featuring birds, formed the subject of the second in the special pictorial series. And a third such series, trumpeting British Technology, followed later. One particular value, the 6d, brought protests from some members of the motor industry. Cars were symbolically represented by two cars, in silhouette, of obvious parentage. As always the Post Office was quite deaf to such vocal utterings and blind to written representations. And the lucky firms sent off envelopes to all their customers, revelling in the free publicity.

As the World Cup fever died down, another bright idea was introduced. The Battle of Hastings, 1066 and all that, was given special treatment. All the designs for the stamps were taken from the famous Bayeux Tapestry, and it was decided to develop six different scenes from the record of the battle. Someone thought that they would look splendid all together, in a se-tenant strip of six across the sheet, and so perhaps they did. Unaccustomed to such an unwieldy shape, the poor collector found that his album could not accommodate them. There was no alternative but to break the strip, or mount them on the slant, both unsatisfactory compromises. At least after this excursion the Post Office promised that it would never be repeated. On the higher values the Queen's head was embossed with foil, giving the appearance of gold. Nine colours were used in printing the 4d sheet, and on some individual stamps, all nine of these colours appeared, breaking another record.

Finally to Christmas, and the first pair of what was to prove to be a popular annual series. Inspiration for the designs were prepared by children as part of a competition, and the two lucky winners, Tasveer Shemza and James Berry, not only collected £20 each but also will always have the pleasure of seeing their names on a British postage stamp, as designers. Despite criticism, it was an idea that worked well once, although repetition could be tedious. They are typical of the many youngster-inspired postage stamps from around the world.

A quieter time was enjoyed by all in 1967. An obligatory pair in honour of the European Free Trade Area attracted little attention, for the 9d and 1s 6d values were used, in the main, on overseas mail. A pleasing series of flowers was in part designed by Rev. W. Keble Martin, who at the age of 89 published in 1965 a book on British Wild Flowers. So soon after publication, he saw 60 years of work become a standard reference book on the subject, and the stamps are public testimony to his skill.

Paintings in July, another special set, followed the worldwide attention focused on such issues by a growing band of theme collectors, who do not collect by country, but by topic or design. 'Master Lambton', a typical eighteenth-century gentleman, is by Sir Thomas Lawrence. 'Mare and Foals in a Landscape', by George Stubbs, was complemented by a modern work, 'Children Coming out of School', by Laurence Lowry RA. This later work is typical of this contemporary artist, who has specialised in north of England industrial scenes.

At the last minute, a single to honour the trip round the world, with just one stop, by Sir Francis Chichester. It features his famous yacht, and he can be seen on board, in miniature, with his typical yachting cap. This was the first time a living Briton, outside the Royal Family, had appeared on a United Kingdom stamp. Be he ever so tiny, he is there. Although the 1s 9d denomination was chosen to limit the printing order, it was immediately popular. Chichester Post Office sold out its entire allocation of 40,000 stamps in 35 minutes. Plymouth, the port of landfall, experienced a queue 300 yards long.

British Scientific Discoveries and a second Christmas series round off the year. In 1967 the Christmas theme was Old Masters, with a Nativity portrayal. This set appeared in two parts: the 4d was issued early to prepay overseas rates, and the 3d and 1s 6d followed six weeks later.

1968 was even quieter. Only four sets, no strange se-tenant strips or funny business. There was but one true commemorative set, covering four different anniversaries in May, each rating one stamp. Two pictorial issues, bridges in April and paintings in August, were followed by the Christmas set in November. The timing of the Christmas stamps continued to cause comment. It was rightly pointed out that they were issued too late for surface mail to far-off parts of the globe, and yet came out too early for internal mail. By the time the average member of the public had got his cards addressed and ready to post, the stamps were sold out.

No sooner was 1968 over than the first of the 1969 barrage hit. It was as though the Post Office had been sleeping for the past two years, to wake with memories of the past. Ships were

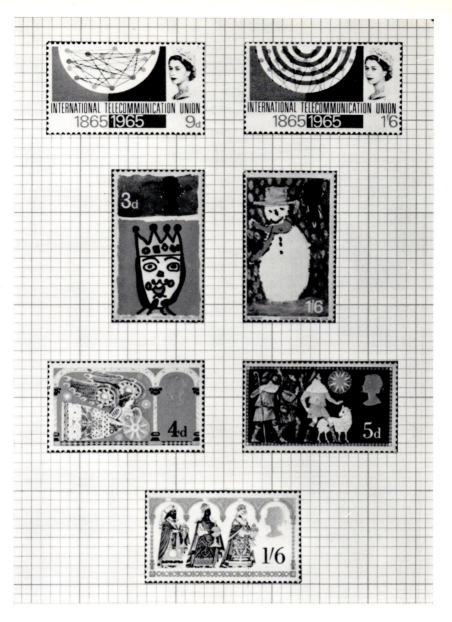

7. COMMEMORATIVE DESIGN
ITU Abstract symbolism
Christmas 1966, and child designed stamps
Christmas 1969, religious themes interpreted by one artist

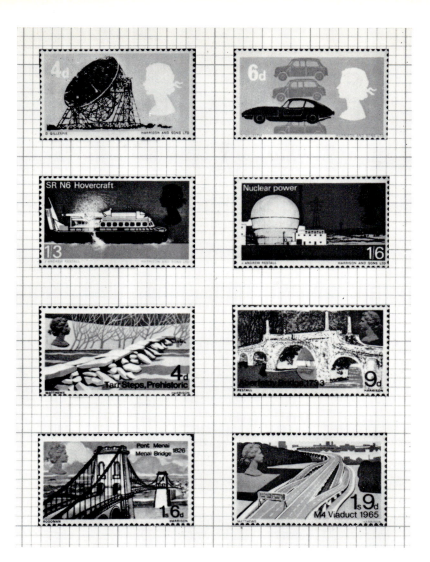

8. PICTORIAL ISSUES

Stamps no longer issued for a particular event or anniversary. The upper set advertises British achievements, and the lower looks at bridges through the ages

the theme, and many of them on 15 January. Originally planned for issue two days later to coincide with the Queen Elizabeth 2 maiden voyage, it was changed through pressure from postal staff, who made the point that Friday was a busy day. It did not matter for the maiden voyage did not start until May. The prestige vessel was given a treble-sized 5d, and old ships took up the remaining stamps. Three double-sized 9d, and two treble-sized 1s stamps all se-tenant completed the fleet.

Concorde, the Anglo-French supersonic airliner, at last got off the ground on 2 March. Supplies of special stamps, printed months before, were to hand for sale as part of the official celebrations. In London they had been held in all post offices for some weeks, with the injunction not to display or sell them until the word was passed along. Originally the idea was to put the stamps on sale on the day of the flight, but most inconsiderately the aircraft took off on a Sunday. So the first day was the following Monday, when simultaneous sale was arranged all over the country. In France they managed to get their stamp out on the Sunday, but only at one office, the rest of the country waiting a few more days.

More anniversaries, five sharing five stamps in April, followed quickly by six cathedrals in May, and the long-awaited celebration for the Investiture of the Prince of Wales at Caernarvon in July. These were somewhat disappointing, for although much trouble had been taken over their production, most of the selected designs were symbolic, rather than modern. Best of the bunch was a portrait of Prince Charles, with his mother's head peering over his hair. Technically the issue was a step forward, as the paper was given a special coat to give a gloss to the silver background. Another unusual feature was that the Caernarvon Castle sections were printed over, instead of under, the phosphor lines to give a three dimensional effect.

The summer ended with a stamp for Mahatma Ghandi in August. This was the first time a set had been issued to honour a Commonwealth citizen.

On 1 October, the great vesting day, the old General Post Office, became the Post Office Corporation. A long-awaited, long-heralded history and achievements set, later described as a history and activities set, was finally issued as a Post Office Technology series. They tried hard with the stamps, but unfortunately, despite all their efforts, the subjects were too abstract for the man in the street. Delacryl, a trade process, was used for the first time in Great Britain, and they were also the first stamps to come from De La Rue. Harrisons contract gave the Post Office freedom to call in other printers for up to two issues each year.

Christmas 1969, and the usual criticisms over the date of issue. At least the new corporation was taking heed of some complaints. A 4d value, now the second-class mail rate, was added to the planned set, in place of a proposed 9d. Excuses for the omission of second-class mail stamps in the past had varied from the difficulty in segregating mail to the technical difficulties of applying a single phosphor line. At least the second explanation proved true, for three quarters of the printing had the lines applied too wide, so that the machines shunted mail with this stamp into the first-class mail pile. Thirty-three stamps in all made this the busiest year to date.

1970, the year before decimal currency was somewhat more restful. It began in February with British Architecture as it was described, although wisely the Post Office confined their attentions to one narrow aspect—cottage architecture. This British Rural series was the work of two designers, David Gentleman and Sheila Robinson, and their different approaches demanded two formats. Diplomatic as a state corporation the four vignettes visited all four sections of the United Kingdom, and the Welsh Stucco was described in English and Welsh.

Five anniversaries were included in the April series. There was some discussion around the events actually selected for commemoration, which is inevitable in a nation so rich in history and institutions. 650 years after the Declaration of Arbroath, this significant landmark in Scottish history was for the first time brought to the attention of all the people of the United Kingdom. Edward II had persuaded the Pope to excommunicate the Scottish King, Robert the Bruce, and this declaration was the Scottish nations answer.

International Cooperative Alliance celebrated their 75th anniversary and the Royal Astronomical Society their 150th. The sailing of the *Mayflower* and Florence Nightingale's 150th birthday were more well-known occasions.

Literary Anniversaries had been promised by the Post Office

for 1970, but in the event they were confined to a single stamp for the 200th birthday of William Wordsworth, and a block of four 5d values for the centenary of the death of Charles Dickens. This later figure was honoured by a number of overseas Commonwealth countries and the four scenes taken from his many books can be supplemented.

After the sixth Commonwealth Games in Wales, the ninth of the series in Edinburgh was a natural for a special set. Designers continually strive for a new approach and J. Andrew Restall succeeded with his 'foot-exposure' camera technique in the series issued on 15 July. Futurist in impact, the stamps convey the impression of athletes in fast motion through formalised images taken from sections of cine film, superimposed in a sequence of movement.

1970 was International year for British philatelists with Great Britain holding its large exhibition of the best in stamps from all over the world. Exhibitions had been held before, but this was the first time a special set of stamps had been included in the festivities. Cooperation from the Post Office was extensive, including a special booklet of stamps, three colour special postmarks for each day, and a large exhibition area within the International show itself. The usual Christmas series completed the programme.

4

The Regionals

Coming from a traditional and ultra-conservative Post Office, the announcement in 1956 that Britain was to have regional issues was a surprise. Even so, they were not the first stamps issued for a particular part of the British Isles. This distinction is claimed by the German Occupation issues of the Channel Islands, whose use was sanctioned by the occupying power. Refusing to use the proposed German swastika overprints, but forced to consider some form of alternative as the British King George VI stocks dried up, the islanders prepared a number of local designs in both Jersey and Guernsey. After the war the British Post Office also sanctioned two special stamps, primarily for sale in the Channel Islands, recalling the liberation. Supplies of these were also placed on sale, by special request, at a few Head Post Offices on the mainland.

In a written answer, Dr Charles Hill, the then Postmaster-General, made the following disclosure on 18 July 1956: 'Her Majesty the Queen has graciously approved in principle the issue of new stamps in the 2½d, 4d and 1s 3d denominations for Scotland, Wales and Northern Ireland, and a 2½d stamp in Jersey, Guernsey and the Isle of Man. The basic design of the stamps will remain unchanged. The head of Her Majesty will continue to be the dominant feature. The border will bear symbols or designs appropriate to the places I have mentioned. I propose to invite committees representing cultural and artistic interests in these areas to advise on detailed designs, for me to submit to Her Majesty on approval. The new stamps will be on sale only in the area which they represent, but they will be

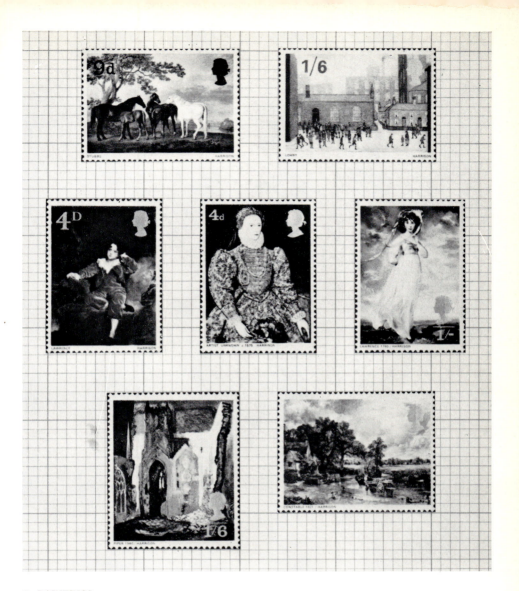

9. PAINTINGS
Paintings are a widely collected theme. The British Post Office
joined in with larger than normal size series

10. REGIONALS

First row: 2½d shortlived values for Guernsey, Jersey, and Isle of Man *Second row:* 4d for same Islands. *Third row:* N. Ireland 5d, Scotland 5d and 6d. *Fourth row:* original three values from Wales valid for postage and revenue purposes throughout the British Isles.'

The announcement was not greeted with unqualified approval. Certain sections of the philatelic press, far from congratulating the authorities on their original and bold step, condemned the idea for the effect it would have on the philatelic reputation of Great Britain. How ideas have changed since those far-off days of 1956!

Heads of art schools, editors of regional magazines, chairmen and presidents of local art councils, representatives of the universities and of the Colleges of Arms were joined together to select a postage stamp. The first function of the committees was to suggest symbols for inclusion in the borders of the new stamps. They were also asked to suggest the names of artists who might be invited to submit new designs. These artists were also to help the Postmaster-General to choose the selected designs.

In the official lists only Lt Col W. Byam, described as an art connoisseur and philatelist, appears as a direct representative of the hobby. There was no reason why collectors should have been chosen, for at that time the postage stamp was considered to be just another art form, without any special problems. Miniscule art was not recognised as a separate field in its own right. Nevertheless, it is generally accepted that the Guernsey design, chosen by the committee to which Lt Col. Byam belonged, is one of the best of the bunch.

Once the terms of reference of the committee were announced, it was clear that symbolism would continue to be a dominant part of British postage stamps. There seemed to be little scope for the impatiently awaited pictorial stamps that so many collectors desired. By June 1957 the committee had ponderously completed their appointed tasks, only later to receive from all sides complaints of the cluttered appearance. The bits and pieces were fitted in wherever opportunity offered. Not until August 1958, 25 months after the initial announcement, did the first regional stamps appear, and the higher values for Wales, Scotland and Northern Ireland were deferred to 29 September that year.

Between the original notification and the date of release, postage rates had risen. Inland letters were charged at 3d from

October 1957, in place of 2½d, and this denomination was accordingly revised. Overseas mail too had been raised from 4d to 6d, so that these values also had to be changed. Only the 1s 3d of the original statement made its planned appearance.

All the Welsh designs were by R. Stone. Each of the three stamps displays the Welsh dragon at the foot, and in addition the 3d and 1s 3d feature the leek, national symbol of Wales. On St David's Day, true Welshman carry the leek proudly in their buttonhole, and it has been cunningly arranged to form a frame on the 3d, while it is placed as a counterbalance to the value tablet on the 1s 3d.

For Scotland's issue there were three designers, and so no uniformity of style. F. Huntley, in his 3d value, incorporated the St Andrew's Cross or Saltire, and Her Majesty's Royal Badge for Scotland, the crowned thistle. J. B. Fleming tackled the 6d in a different way: thistles and their leaves are arranged to form a decorative frame. A. B. Imrie was more formal, using the supporters of the Scottish Royal Coat-of-Arms for the 1s 3d.

Northern Ireland also called on the services of three designers. W. Hollywood fitted in the Ulster Right Hand, as used on the seal of the O'Neills, Kings of Ulster, and two sprays of flax, in recognition of the importance to the province of the linen industry. L. Pilton also used the flax symbolically and for a balancing effect inserted two right hands on either side of the 6d value. This is the only stamp in the series with an ornamental background. The Queen's head is poised on a linen woven diamond pattern. T. Collins also considered the hand and flax essential, and added a field gate, with its typical Ulster stone-supporting posts.

The three islands had to be content with a single 3d stamp, one in each region. E. A. Piprell included a Guernsey lily and the crown of William the Conqueror in his Guernsey design. Taken from a silver penny coin of the reign of William I, Duke of Normandy, the crown is a silent reminder that Guernsey formed part of the Norman domains, long before they invaded England.

Royal symbols were also chosen by W. M. Gardener. The Royal Mace of Jersey, presented to the island in 1663 by Charles I and the coat-of-arms granted by Edward I in 1279 support a floral background, confirming the position of the island as a supplier of flowers and fruit.

J. H. Nicholson cleverly incorporated the legs of Man, the Celtic badge of the island, and a Celtic ring chain border, to make up the Isle of Man value. All these stamps had, as promised by the Postmaster-General, the Dorothy Wilding portrait of the Queen for their central feature.

It is still not clear why the first day of release was split into two for the 12 stamps. All the 3d values were placed on sale from 18 August 1958, and the 6d and 1s 3d denominations followed on 29 September. It has been suggested that the Post Office had taken this course to make it a little easier for philatelists and the stamp trade. This does not ring true, for on more than one occasion three and even four stamps had been issued at the same time. These regional stamps were available only in their respective regions, so even with simultaneous release, no more than three stamps would have been involved in one place, on one day. Certainly no further acts of cooperation were forthcoming. No special covers, no distinctive postmarks, to grace the enterprise. Only privately produced printed envelopes were serviced, but their clean, clear postmarks indicate that at least the Post Office had issued instructions for careful handling.

All the stamps appeared on the new all-over Crown watermark, and it is possible that the change was prompted from political motives. It would hardly have been seemly to upset the strong wave of Scottish Nationalism, with special Scottish stamps printed on paper reading Elizabeth the *Second*.

Originally the 12 stamps were issued on the then usual cream paper. Later the Post Office announced the switch to white stock, although, as with the definitives, there are difficulties in allocating copies to their correct printings. Nevertheless the authorities carefully informed the collecting world of every new release. It was a pity that they were not so helpful as new gum was introduced, or when the far more important phosphor line and watermark changes were placed on sale some years later.

In 1963 an announced special printing was made for the Isle of Man, 3d, on coated paper, a residual stock first used for the 1960 Europa commemoratives. This was one of a long series of paper experiments that have continued, mostly in secrecy, up to the present day. An unsolved mystery, despite many articles and prolonged correspondence, concerns the date of issue of this variety. It is either 17 May or 15 July 1963. It is also possible that they were first placed on sale, not on the island, but at the Philatelic Bureau.

The opening of the Bureau on 1 May 1963 made the regionals much easier to obtain. Previously they had only been freely available, outside the countries concerned, at exhibition post offices. Earlier in the year the Automatic Letter Facing machines had been installed at Glasgow. Scottish regionals in the city, and the surrounding area, were available with blue phosphor lines. The opportune opening of the Bureau simplified collection of these experimental varieties.

It was all very well for the large regions, but the islands repeatedly made the point that not only were they restricted to a single 3d stamp, but also that most visitors sent postcards home. These came under a $2\frac{1}{2}$ rate. After continued pressure, three $2\frac{1}{2}$d stamps were placed on sale from 8 June 1964, in Guernsey, Jersey and the Isle of Man.

Only Jersey called in a new designer, E. Blampied, who managed to find room for the ER cypher in addition to all the other essential elements. Otherwise it was a simple case of rearrangement of the basic material. For one long summer season these stamps were used in their millions. By the time the following tourist season came round, postcards cost 3d. After all the fuss they need not have bothered!

Keeping in step with 3d postcards, letters advanced to 4d, and all the regions were left without a basic stamp. In Scotland the 3d now met the printed postage rate, and was reissued with one phosphor line in place of two. Originally the lines were placed down the vertical perforations, to either the right or to the left, producing two collectable varieties. It was generally agreed that the Dorothy Wilding portrait had outlived its time, and new designs were being considered. But as a temporary stop-gap, 4d denominations would appear, at first in the old 3d designs.

Seven 4d stamps were placed on sale in the six regions on 7 February 1966. Scotland collected two versions, with and without phosphor lines. The substance was violet phosphor, and the 3d, 6d and 1s 3d were issued with the new treatment at

11. HIGH VALUES
The long-lived Castles series, The Machin Head £1 with plate number

12. POSTAGE DUES

Long-lived uniform utilitarian design for denoting postage due.
The values from 2s 6d to £1 are inscribed 'To Pay'. This design was
replaced in 1970, when the first decimal denominations appeared

about the same time.

Further rises in foreign postage rates came into force on 3 October 1966. It became necessary to replace the 6d and 1s 3d values by 9d and 1s 6d denominations. These were the days of Post Office stock rationalisation, and so the new stamps were printed with phosphor bands only.

This same policy meant changes on all fronts. The 6d and 1s 3d were sold to exhaustion, and 3d stamps were reissued with phosphor bands, placed centrally. Later the 4d values were released with lines too. Two other changes in the finished form led philatelists a merry chase for a few months. Unwatermarked paper was introduced and the new PVA gum was used. One after another, new varieties appeared, with the Post Office proving most uncooperative. New releases went unheralded, new issues remained unknown. In one case, the Northern Ireland 4d with PVA gum, the stamp was released only at a few philatelic counters, after it had been withdrawn from all offices in Ulster itself. Petulantly stating that gum changes were unimportant, in marked contrast to its opinion on the status of white paper printings, the Post Office ordered the withdrawal of all stocks. Not important, but serious enough to stop selling such stamps.

Two-tier postage called for a 5d value. The same stale super-annuated design was brought out again, and the opportunity was taken to bring the 4d colour in line with the new definitives. 4d sepia one band and 5d blue two bands, for all six regions, were placed on sale from 4 September 1968. Interest focused on the stamps of Jersey and Guernsey, for it had already been announced that these islands would run their own postal affairs from 1 October 1969. A life of just over 12 months seemed brief enough, but it was to be shorter still. From 26 February 1969 the 4d went red, to aid the sorter in his division of first- and second-class mail.

Jersey and Guernsey stamps were withdrawn on 1 October 1969, and the two islands issued their own stamps. But the regionals remained valid for postage elsewhere in the United Kingdom and the Isle of Man. Strange indeed that they could be invalid in the planned place of issue, but acceptable in other countries.

Current 9d and 1s 6d denominations, as the printings became exhausted, were reissued on unwatermarked paper. First to go was the Scotland 1s 6d, followed by the same value in Northern Ireland and Wales. Demand for the 9d stamp ran at roughly half the 1s 6d consumption rate.

First-day postmarks, with the envelope slogan, were introduced with the 2½d, and were also provided for some later issues. Official souvenir envelopes and circular handstamps were provided for the 4d sepia, 5d blue combination, but no facilities were available for the phosphor and watermark changes, or for the 4d red issue. Some of the new issues received the full blast of Post Office publicity, including slogan postmarks in principal towns heralding forthcoming additions.

Regional decimal values in new designs were announced in 1970, bringing the long period of Wilding portraits to an end.

5

The High Values

The British Post Office has always been unusually proud of its choices for high value stamps. A separate contract had been held by Waterlow and Sons from 1934 for the denominations between 2s 6d and £1. While the demand for some of the lower values was practically insatiable, above 2s 6d sales were much smaller, so that these expensive stamps could be produced by a more elaborate process. Line engraving, or recess, uses the principle that ink lies in the hollows or recesses of the plate, which is then forced onto the paper under pressure. By skilful engraving, dots, lines and hatching present an impression of delicate shading and hues.

Dr Charles Hill, Postmaster-General on 31 August 1955, well-known as the one-time Radio Doctor, brought his little black bag along to a press conference. From it he extracted the new stamps, representing the Elizabethan age. Two of them, 10s and £1, were to be issued the very next day, and the 2s 6d and 5s followed on 23 September.

The Postmaster-General had called upon the services of an advisory panel, a committee in the best traditions of the civil service. For once they seem to have selected a design acceptable to a wide body of opinion. They had chosen the work of Mr Lynton Lamb.

Lynton Lamb, a painter in oil and water colour, designer and illustrator in wood engraving, had at that time illustrated several books, and designed the binding of the Bible used at the Queen's Coronation. His previous work for the Post Office included the composition of the Coronation greetings telegram form.

Mr Lamb had chosen four castles of the United Kingdom, each representative, in its way, of the separate and common traditions of the four quarters of the Kingdom. For the 2s 6d in brown, Carrickfergus Castle, on the shores of Belfast Lough. To Wales, and the famous Caernarvon Castle, pictured on the 5s red, birthplace of Edward II, first Prince of Wales, and later to be the scene of the Investiture to that title of Prince Charles. Edinburgh Castle, chosen for the 10s blue, includes part of the one-time Royal Palace of the Kings of Scotland. Pride of place went to Windsor Castle, home and haven for the Royal Family, especially at Christmas time. This was the choice for the £1 black. Carefully selected to represent the peoples of the United Kingdom, the stamps appear to have been allocated in strict order, matching the size of population of each country in turn. While fitting perhaps that Windsor should occupy the highest denomination, it is in some ways a pity. Even with the inflating postage rates, it is a rare internal letter that carries over a pound's worth of postage, and inland parcels never do. Most non-collectors have never seen it, and are blithely unaware that such a stamp even exists. Of course they are used, in their hundreds of thousands, on overseas parcels and airmail letters.

Each castle is shown through a common frame, a 'broken grotto' or window, and in the side panel, a Wilding portrait of the Queen. This is a different photograph from the one chosen for the small-size definitives.

These stamps appeared on the St Edward's crown watermark paper, although they were not the first to be issued thus. A few of the lower values had just made their debut. No less than six distinct issues of the high value castle were to appear in the 15 years' life of the set.

First of the changes, producing the second issue, occurred in 1958. From 1 January 1958 the printing contract at long last left Waterlow and Sons, as part of the regular five years review. It was handed over to De La Rue, who also received the printing plates. Philatelists collect both printings, but they are far from easy to distinguish. Since the price tag for the second printing is roughly three times as great as the first, it is well worth taking some trouble to allocate them correctly.

Complete sheets offer little difficulty, for the marginal

markings are quite different. It is in single copies, both mint and used, that bring the problems. Without any qualification, the foolproof method is to compare copies with those whose pedigrees have already been established. Otherwise, the general impression must be the guide. Early Waterlow printings were on creamy paper, and this assigns such stamps without dispute. The width of the gutters between frames may help if the stamps are in pairs. All Waterlow printings were between 3.8 and 4mm apart horizontally, and up to 4.5mm vertically. Corresponding measurements for the first De La Rue issues are 3.4 to 3.8mm, and 4.5 to 4.6mm respectively. Later De La Rue printings are less certain in these dimensions. One final test, that often settles the question conclusively, is to examine the design itself. Waterlow printings are characterised by whiskers and extraneous lines of colour. De La Rue, on the other hand, tends to produce a clearer, cleaner impression, and the colours are softer, warmer and lighter.

De La Rue stamps were introduced gradually between May and August 1958, to be replaced in less than a year by printings on new watermark paper. This is one explanation for the high price of the first De La Rue set. A second, more pertinent reason, is that many collectors just ignored the new stamps, content in their belief that there was little worthwhile difference. How wrong they were! Only later, after exhaustive specialist attention, did they wake up, to find no stocks left. All-over crown watermark printings were placed on sale between June and July 1959, and remained available for about four years. Towards the end of the run, a new white paper was in use, but they are not clearly distinguishable to the naked eye. Ultra-violet fluorescent reactions are the only safe measures for separation.

At the close of the five-year period the contract was again transferred, this time to Bradbury, Wilkinson. Although the same watermark continued in use, distinguishing between the work of the two printers is relatively simple. In complete sheets all Bradbury, Wilkinson printings bear a plate number, in the lower margin to the right; this consists of a number or a number and letter. Apart from the £1, colours are clearly different; sepia instead of blackish brown, scarlet rather than rose-red, and bright in place of dull blue give a positive shade guide. In all cases the design is much heavier, most noticeable in the diadem and the lines of shading on the face.

Nine different plates were used for the 2s 6d, and four for the 5s. Later printings did not always match tints, and a specialised collection can present a wide range. In error both 2s 6d and 5s were issued on inverted watermark paper, and these are rare. One unusual error, purchased in Birmingham, consisted of a complete sheet of 5s stamps, printed on the gummed side. Before the lucky purchaser had woken up to the importance of the find, ten copies had been used on mail.

One surprise, towards the end of the run of castle stamps, was their reissue on paper without watermark. New designs and new stamps had been promised, but technical delays had brought postponements. As a temporary measure, all stamps were printed on this paper, and issued at post offices, the £1 as early as December 1967, and the 2s 6d completed the set in July 1968. For once, the £1 appeared in a distinct shade of black.

An experimental special printing was made of all four of the high values on coated watermark paper, but only the 2s 6d was issued. It was officially stated that the results of this exploration were unsatisfactory, and stocks of the remaining denominations were destroyed. Only 60,000 sheets of the 2s 6d were sold, a total of under two and a half million stamps, but it was heavily bought. It remains common.

After postponement and speculation, at long last, on 5 March 1969, the Machin Head version was placed on sale. Remaining stocks of the old castles were sold to exhaustion, with a reserve available from the Philatelic Bureau. In Wales, the Caernarvon Castle 5s was specially retained, for collectors wishing to tie in the theme, with the many commemorative postmarks arranged as part of the festivities for the Investiture of the Prince of Wales. All four values were withdrawn on 15 May 1970, remaining valid for postage, until demonetised, as part of the decimal programme.

6

The Machin Heads

Acclaimed as one of the best designs of all time, the Machin Head series made an impact as soon as the first stamps were issued in 1967. They are examples of classic simplicity, the hallmark of a great stamp. First appearing in June 1967, they have been so well received that they have continued with an extended lease of life into the decimal era.

It was in March 1967 that the Postmaster-General revealed the official choice for the new series. He called it 'a classic of stamp history, one of the greatest stamps of all time'. The origin of the simple, yet adequate composition, was a photograph of the Queen, taken by her brother-in-law, Lord Snowdon. He took many portraits, but one was destined to become the most familiar likeness, with millions of copies sold every day. From the picture, Arnold Machin, OBE, RA, prepared side-face sculptural busts. Then on a foggy morning when the light was just right, a photographer from the High Wycombe works of Harrisons captured the delicate lines of the moulding. One photograph was perfect for the stamp.

Mr Machin had made six bas-relief portraits in all, before the final one was chosen. Essays and trials galore were prepared, many of them reduced to stamp size, and then printed by photogravure, to judge the finished effect. Various sizes of the portrait, many positions and styles of the wording were examined. Not until the last minute was the decision made to cut out the words altogether. This master stroke was the elusive touch needed.

Every country, except Britain, must by Universal Postal Union regulations, include their territorial name. Britain is exempt, not by prescription, but by long-honoured custom, as a tribute to the first country to issue an adhesive postage stamp. But also by tradition, it is considered necessary to include the sovereign's head, as an indication of origin. So when the design was simplified to portrait and denomination the two essentials were there—origin and value.

The fascinating stages of preparation were the centrepiece of an exhibition held in the National Postal Museum. Three of the sculptured heads, and many frames of the essays and postage-stamp size proofs and trials were on display, tracing the ideas of the artists as they strove for perfection. Many long months elapsed before the happy result blended into form. For serious students, the material is now in the Museum's archives, to be studied at leisure.

The head agreed, the next stage was to complete the artwork. All that remained was to position the value, and, as with the Wilding portraits before, this was no simple task. Many positions were tried, many sizes of figures tentatively offered, before each value became acceptable. To appreciate the difficulty, compare the amount of space taken up by '1d' and '1/9'. Three stamps, 7d, 8d and 9d, have the figures placed to the right of the portrait, instead of at the left.

Colours had to be chosen, once the design was settled. Sufficient contrast within the series was essential to prevent confusion between different values. The Queen herself selected the colour for the basic letter rate of 4d. Accepting the design without any reservations, she chose olive-brown sepia. In the printers' own description, the 1s stamp appeared in aconite violet, and the 1s 9d denomination in tangerine orange and olive brown.

All the stamps were expected to enjoy a long life. No reasons for any immediate change were expressed. Nevertheless wise and wary collectors bought their copies immediately they were issued—always a sensible system. This forethought paid dividends, for changes there were to be, and many of them.

All this was in the future on 5 June 1967, when the first three denominations were placed on sale. To accompany the new stamps, a very simple first-day cover envelope was prepared by the Post Office, and a neat small handstamp was employed at all offices with philatelic posting boxes. An informative stiffener, giving details of the set, referred readers to the Post

Office *Philatelic Bulletin.*

1s 9d was a new denomination, introduced to meet the air-mail rate to the Far East, Australasia and Oceania. It was not the first time a definitive had been issued in more than one colour, but it is necessary to travel back to 1910 to locate a predecessor.

No watermark and all phosphor lined simplified the series; it looked as though nothing could go wrong. Plain paper eliminated all the watermark varieties, but the phosphor bands proved to be another story. On the one hand there were the specimens with no phosphor lines at all. Some denominations exist in large quantities, and others have only been discovered in very small handfuls. Immediately popular, the chase was on. A catalogue appeared listing all the missing phosphor errors, and the complete definitive set could be purchased without lines, at a price.

To complicate matters further, the original stamps appear to have had the lines applied by a variety of means. Photogravure has been noted, with a screen of either 150 or 250, the figures expressing the number of dots to the inch. And flexograph, a sort of rubber stereo application, has been discovered on some values.

A second instalment, on 8 August 1967, was made up of 3d violet, 9d deep green, and 1s 6d turquoise and blue. This completed the 1967 releases. The 4d stamps seemed to be devoured by the public at an insatiable rate, and printing followed printing. Before long there was a comprehensive range of shades to choose from, as difficulties emerged in colour matching.

Booklets and coils presented further colour variations. Later printings of many denominations achieved catalogue status.

An exciting error, almost fated to happen, involved the bicoloured 1s 6d. A full sheet was found with light blue missing. A London dealer offered them at £60 for a block of four stamps.

First of many changes came when least expected: the gum was altered. For many years all British stamps had been prepared with gum arabic. This is a natural exudate from acacia trees in Africa, and it had become increasingly difficult to obtain. The best gum arabic must be several years old, and the stocks of the old crop were diminishing. Looking ahead, Harrisons had been in close collaboration with the Post Office, searching for an alternative. After extensive tests and field trials, a synthetic adhesive was invented. Completely non-toxic, colourless, odourless and tasteless, it is known as Polyvinyl Alcohol, and familiarly named PVA by philatelists. Delivered in powder form from the factory, it is then processed and developed by a trade formula. As a liquid it is applied to paper in the usual way. In spite of its name, the PVA gum has no taste, and it is invisible, so a small amount of pale yellowish colouring matter is added to make it visible, so that the printers can check that the paper has been gummed.

The popular 4d was first to appear. Next the third instalment of the definitives, $\frac{1}{2}$d orange, 1d olive bistre, 2d red brown and 6d magenta, all on 5 February 1968. Lastly, the fourth and final instalment of the low values was released on 1 July 1968, namely the 5d Stuart blue, 7d light green, 8d scarlet, and 10d light brown.

All these stamps were issued on surfaced paper. A few copies of the 10d on unsurfaced paper, similar to the 1953 definitives, but without watermark, were found in 1970. It is thought that Harrisons, who surface their own reels, failed to complete the treatment towards the end of one roll, by error.

Phosphor lines are supposed to excite the optical scanning system of ALF. Two lines indicate ordinary mail, and one line second-class mail at the basic rate. Cheap postage for this last class has always been allowed on the understanding that mail could be delayed. Initially the 3d was printed with one band, so that the machine could recognise packages prepaid at the then printed paper rate.

Two-tier postage was introduced on 16 September 1968. A radical new principle, differentiating between the speed of service required, came to stay. No longer was mail judged on its contents, but on its urgency, and new postage rates were devised at the same time. Basic first-class mail cost 5d, and second-class 4d. New arrangements of phosphor lines were needed, and a new printing of 4d sepia with one line was made. Issued in advance, with instructions not to sell them before 16 September, large stocks were sent to all offices.

Complaints came flooding in from sorting-office staff, who had to make the new scheme work. Many of the letters had to be segregated on the sorting tables, under artificial light.

Under certain conditions, it was apparently difficult to distinguish between sepia and blue, the respective colours of the 4d and 5d. The much publicised Queen's choice was cast aside, and in its place came the 4d red. This in turn required a change in colour for the 8d, which was switched to turquoise blue. Naturally the new 4d had one band, and was recognised by collectors as a distinct stamp. The Post Office did not feel able to offer first-day cover services for either the 4d sepia one band, or for the new colours 4d and 8d, issued on 6 January 1969. Shortage of time, and the difficulties in effecting nationwide distribution, were their alibis.

Other changes were also noted, mostly unheralded. Sharp-eyed collectors were the first to discover them. It was expected that the 3d would revert to two phosphor bands, and it was already known from certain booklets. Eventually they did appear.

The 2s coin-in-the-slot booklets were providing their own variations. At first containing four 4d, and two each of 1d and 3d se-tenant, all stamps were treated with two bands. Later in September 1968 the contents were changed to six 4d stamps, one pane of four, and one pane of two se-tenant with an advertisement label. This later form first appeared in sepia, and then in red.

Other booklets were exciting attention. Following the revision of postage rates, the 10s edition was completely restyled, and contained one pane of six, four at 1d and two at 4d, se-tenant, in addition to more conventional sheets. All six stamps were printed with only one band, the first time that the 1d had been issued so. Only one edition of this booklet was sold, and then it was replaced by a 4d red in January. In this form, 1d stamps reverted to two lines, and the 4d red had one line, not applied centrally, but at the left side. One final variation came from the Cook booklet. This was another of the Post Office's experiments, to see if they could create a sale for a high-priced booklet. All the panes contain 15 stamps, with attached recipes, and the interleaves contain further cookery hints, and dishes in full, mouth-watering colour. One of these panes is made up in an unusual composition, namely 4d + 1d + 5d + 1d + 4d; the two end stamps of each row are one line at left or right respectively.

Se-tenant panes are comparatively difficult to find. Should a dealer wish to put by a large stock, he has to buy complete booklets, and then dispose of the remaining values as best he can. Many of the panes will be trimmed, so that full perforation panes are worth a fair premium.

27 August 1969 saw strange sights at a few selected post offices scattered around the country. Britain's first multi-value coils were on sale from new vending machines. It all happened in a bit of a hurry, with even the philatelic services section of the Post Office taken by surprise. On the first day the machines were in use every minute, and the special counters had supplies of the stamps on sale, over the counter, the first time this concession had been granted. Normally, coils are available only in complete reels. It was all rather unofficial, in a bid to speed up sales. Queues at the counter, to buy by the strip, and queues at the machines, to feed one-shilling pieces into the mechanism took many hours to disperse. All five stamps, 2d + 2d + 3d + 1d + 4d, had but one central line, and surprisingly were with the old gum arabic.

Neatly fitting in with the National Stamp Exhibition, the long-awaited new high values appeared on 5 March 1969: 2s 6d, 5s, 10s, and £1, it was soon clear that there were four panes to the master sheet, lettered for instance 1, 1A, 1B and 1C. Conclusions, swiftly drawn, that all combinations existed, were soon proved to be false. Not only were some numbers missing entirely, but also some letter combinations for issued numbers were not to be found. Early journal and catalogue entries are in some cases wrong, and although later corrected, emphasise the importance of consulting up-to-date works of reference. Missing numbers were allocated to plates not up to standard, and withdrawn by the printers. First planned some six months earlier, these high values had been delayed, and in part the missing plates explain this interval.

A Post Office First-Day Cover service was available, and no charge was made if the envelope carried sufficient postage. The complete set was serviced for the cost of the envelope and the stamps, and so they might! Nearly £2 for an inland letter is a little over the odds, by any standard. Special handling of covers at all stages of their journey, brought almost universal satisfaction.

Presentation packs of the four high values, and of the lower denominations, were included in the permanent range of items available from the Philatelic Bureau, and at some main offices too.

Two types of the 2d were spotted by variety-conscious collectors. In type 1, the figures are further from the left-hand border than in type 2.

After an almost non-existent life, the ½d stamp was withdrawn from general sale on 30 June 1969. Practically the only use for such an insignificant amount was as a make-up on letters posted in travelling post offices, where the first-class postage was supplemented by a halfpenny late fee. This was increased to one penny, when the halfpenny coin was demonetised. On 10 December 1969, the 1s 6d was placed on sale with an all-over phosphor coating. Since the coating is continuous, at first glance these stamps may be confused with the phosphor omitted variety, but the appearance of the paper is rather different. 140,000 sheets, or around 33 million stamps, were printed for test purposes, representing three months' normal sale.

Britain's first decimal postage stamps were issued on 17 June 1970. The central motif of the three denominations, 10p, 20p and 50p, remained unchanged, but the head was moved slightly to the right to accommodate the decimal figures of value. To avoid confusion with the 2s 6d and 5s stamps which remained valid for postage, the 10p was printed in cerise and the 20p in olive green. As the 50p represented exactly 10s, blue was retained. All three decimal high values, and the £1 which continued unchanged, were produced 100 to a sheet, instead of the earlier 40 to a sheet.

The use of one single design throughout the whole range of current stamps is unusual, and the only British precedent was in 1840, when the two solitary values, 1d black and 2d blue, were first issued. Two different methods of printing make the comparison between them a worthwhile exercise. Two different formats open avenues of speculation concerning the most convenient size for a stamp, from both commercial and artistic standpoints. The decision to continue this successful design into the decimal period was greeted on all sides with sighs of relief. Without any doubt Britain's simple definitive stamps satisfy nearly everyone.

7

Postage Due

'Something to pay on this one' is a greeting that most of us have experienced from time to time. And sitting on the cover is an old-fashioned, rather ugly label, glaring out the amount due.

Stamps to collect the postage due on underpaid letters are the only special-purpose types issued by the Post Office. They do not agree that this is so, making their laboured point, time after time, that they are simply accounting labels. Even today, on the Philatelic Bureau's 'Stock List and Order Form', they are described as Postage Due Labels.

From 1914 to 1970 there was only the one basic design in use. The introduction of postage due stamps, to indicate the surcharge on letters posted unpaid or underpaid, was first recommended by the British Post Office in 1912. Not only letters, but also parcels were brought within the scheme. Customs charges, for small amounts, could also be collected in this way.

It was not until April 1914 that the scheme was finally launched. The Postmaster-General was satisfied that their use would provide substantial savings in the collection of small sums. On 20 April 1914 notice was given that 'No surcharges should be paid on the delivery of any letter, parcel or other postal packet, unless it bears a "Postage Due" label or labels to the face value of the amount demanded'. Four denominations were originally issued. G. W. Eve was the designer, and the colours selected were $\frac{1}{2}$d green, 1d carmine, 2d agate, and 5d fawn. Agate was chosen for the 2d label because this was to be the most used value, and the colour was quite distinct from any other British postage stamp at that time. Each label bore the words 'Postage Due', and the face value, in figures centrally, and in words at the foot.

Higher values were soon needed. Parcels returned from abroad attracted substantial fees. Additions to the series were the 1s label in Royal Blue (for its pleasing and distinctive appearance) in 1915 and, following a change in postage rates, a 3d violet in 1918. This low-value series was completed by a 4d grey-green in 1920, and a 1½d brown in 1922. The odd halfpennies are puzzling at first for it is generally known that postage due is twice the normal unpaid postage. At first this odd denomination was needed for the increasing amount of wrongly franked mail from abroad that was chargeable at 1½d on conversion into sterling. This 1½d label had a short life, and was withdrawn in 1925.

First of the high-value labels was brought into use in 1924, mainly for customs and parcels. Instead of 'Postage Due' they are inscribed 'To Pay', and are printed on tinted paper. This 2s 6d stamp was issued in purple on lemon paper.

Early issues were printed by Harrison and Sons, to be replaced by Waterlow in 1924, who in turn were displaced by Harrison in 1936. Four watermarks were in use before the Elizabethan era. Basically they consist of the current Royal Cypher, G V R in two forms, E 8 R, G V I R, and the crown. They are printed sideways in the sheets, and there are many examples with watermark inverted or reversed.

In 1951 some of the colours were changed to match the definitive series. Those affected were ½d, 1d, 4d and 1s, becoming orange, dark blue, light blue and amber respectively. The 1½d returned to the series, this time in green.

It will be seen that many labels, identical in design to those about to be described, belong properly to an earlier period. They are distinguishable only by watermarks, for they are printed from the same plates, and by the same method, typography, as the earlier issues.

It was a matter of little importance to the Post Office that these labels were in use well into 1956 on the old watermarked paper. They were virtually indistinguishable. First to be reported on the Tudor watermark was the 2s 6d in December 1954. This was followed in 1955 by ½d, 2d, 3d, 4d and 5d. A complete sheet of the 4d was discovered at Ewell Post Office in Surrey, lacking all perforations, and found its way onto the market. Standing regulations quite specifically state that faulty stamps must be returned to the Supplies Department, and this leak incurred official displeasure. Nevertheless 120 imperforate pairs are now available, fetching about £40 per pair. Despite their undoubted rarity, they are not sought after because of the irregular method of issue.

Before the series could be completed, there was a watermark change to St Edward's Crown. A new higher value, 5s scarlet on lemon, led the way on 15 November 1955. The remainder, including those not represented by the Tudor series, were on sale in the next seven months, with one exception. Demand for the 2s 6d fell away, after the 5s appeared, and it was not released until June 1957.

Crown watermarked stamps trickled in from 1959, and in most cases were later issued on the white paper. A demand arose after the inland letter rate was increased to 3d, and another new denomination, 6d purple, was made available from 29 March 1962. Mainly for customs fees, two high values, 10s blue and £1 black, both on lemon paper, were added to the range on 2 September 1963. Conversely, the 1½d was withdrawn, with no further supplies sent to post offices from 31 January 1965, and it was removed from sale altogether on 26 April that year.

Eventually the watermarked paper ran out, and both the 2d and 4d were issued in 1968 unwatermarked, with gum arabic. Almost immediately they were followed by 3d, 5d, 6d and 1s but with PVA gum. A demand for an 8d value had been created when letter postage was increased to 4d. Issued on 3 October 1968, it provided an unexpected surprise, for the 8d red was found to have been printed by photogravure. After years of typography, a change in the twilight days of the set, unforeseen. These un-lovely stamps have run their course. Decimal denominations are in a new design, and 56 years of faithful service has come to an end.

For the specialist, the Elizabethan watermarks provide un-limited opportunities to specialise. They may be found reversed, as the paper can be fed into the printing machine the wrong way round. The 1½d has the unusual stop variety, an extraneous mark after the word 'three'.

In addition to the imperforate error, there are a number of unofficial provisionals. On 7 June 1952, the Bury St Edmunds office ran out of 1d postage due labels. Two unofficial hand-stamps were prepared on the authority of the local postmaster, and applied to the then current 1d King George VI definitive. Valued at around £30, the hundred or so copies must rank as the first Queen Elizabeth stamps of Great Britain, albeit that they show the old king's head. But they are unofficial, because local postmasters are not delegated authority to make overprints of this nature.

Camberley ran out of $\frac{1}{2}$d and 1$\frac{1}{2}$d stamps, when a large volume of returned circulars arrived, for return to the Staff College there. Printed matter may for a variety of reasons prove to be un-deliverable, and is then destroyed. However, a written or printed request on the envelope for its return is honoured, and a second postage becomes payable. At the time the rate was 1$\frac{1}{2}$d, and the local solution to the lack of stocks was to bisect the 1d postage due.

Stanley Gibbons noted similar bisected labels in June 1956, when a couple of examples turned up on their own mail. Un-fortunately they were not postmarked, so reducing their interest. Bisected stamps must be tied to a cover by a postmark, or their authenticity is open to doubt. Without an irreproachable pedi-gree they could be easily manufactured.

Apart from the issued stamps, there are a number of colour trials in circulation. They always appear on King George V watermarked paper and so fall outside the scope of this book. But they are comparatively rare and make an interesting intro-duction to the series.

High-value postage due labels in decimal denominations were introduced on 17 June 1970. The denominations, 10p, 20p, 50p and £1, replaced the old 2s 6d to £1 designs. These new decimal 'To Pay' labels came in a new look design by Jeffery Matthews. The colours match the corresponding postage series. In contrast to the earlier ornate stamps, they show simply the figures of value, and the inscription 'To Pay'.

After countless years in the doldrums, the increase in demand for all Great Britain stamps reached postage due labels in 1969. Overnight prices rocketed as their true scarcity was generally recognised. Today the prices reflect this upsurge, but they are still comparatively cheap compared with ordinary postage stamps.

8

Booklets

Why collect booklets? Why bother with them at all? The British Post Office is convinced that they are well worth all the trouble and expense involved in preparing and printing them. It continuously mounts campaigns, aimed at the man in the street, and the housewife at home, persuading them to keep a booklet handy. Selling stamps is a time-consuming task; buying them in dozens or twenties makes sound economic sense and reduces the queue at the counter. But stamps are small and sticky shapes, easily lost or stuck together. Packaging is the answer, preferably in a convenient and attractive form—the booklet. In the early days, back in 1904, an extra halfpenny was charged for the booklet, 24 penny stamps costing 2s $0\frac{1}{2}$d. Later the contents were changed, and the value and cost reduced by the odd half-penny to a round two shillings. Not until 1911 did they decide to bear the extra printing costs themselves, writing off their expenses against the saving of man-hours in the post offices.

So much for the official reasons, but why should this affect a collector? Many, probably the majority, have managed to ignore their very existence without any sense of loss. Collecting is more than the simple exercise of accumulating one of everything. True collectors study a stamp, not necessarily disecting it, bit by bit, but at least forming a representative group, including watermarks and types. They were hardly encouraged by the main catalogue publishers. Over the years the watermark inverted stamp was steadfastly ignored. Only at the beginning of the present reign was a tentative booklet listing printed, and its continuation was in doubt more than once. Watermark inverted varieties first gained a place in the less widely used *Commonwealth Queen Elizabeth Catalogue*. Today, both Stanley Gibbons and the Commonwealth list these varieties in their Elizabethan editions, and from this respectability, and pedigree, the search for booklets is on.

Booklets are complicated to produce. The Post Office must use a special printing cylinder, in order that the familiar booklet form may be produced. Instead of a normal sheet of 240 stamps, a new format is prepared. Consisting of rows of 24 stamps, these are broken every sixth stamp by an unprinted gutter. In each strip of six stamps, three will be upright, and the next three inverted. The sheet, which at one time had 20 rows, is now continuous, printed from a cylinder with 21 rows. When the stamps are separated by a guillotine, they are cut vertically between the third and fourth stamp of each strip of six. Otherwise there would be a major error, *tête-bêche*, one stamp inverted in relation to its fellow. Further cutting along the gutters provides, with the margins, a backing. This procedure permits all panes to be bound at the left, with the stamps upright within the covers.

Watermarked paper was used exclusively for the earlier Elizabethan stamps, and those printed inverted will apparently have the watermark upside down. Roughly equal numbers will exist, normal and inverted, after spoilt copies have been destroyed, and these are the only source of inverted watermark varieties on the definitive low-value stamps.

Booklets are produced in hundreds of thousands, and widely used, so any large accumulation of used stamps on paper from commercial sources will yield a fair number of inverted watermark copies. Until the catalogue listing, few collectors bothered to save complete booklets, and comprehensive collections are thin on the ground.

A representative selection is not too difficult to form. Even with the material to hand, the problem of how to mount and display them remains. There seems little point in hiding them away in a box, never to see the light of day, yet leaf after album leaf of apparently identical booklets, with only covers visible, is hardly an inspiring picture.

A typical simplified collection will aim at one of each form of booklet. A new form is recognised as either a change in contents or a radical change to the form or colour of the cover. More specialised ranges aim at one of each edition, usually dated, and perhaps even duplicated copies covering all watermark varieties. Unfortunately it is not unusual to find the successive sheets to have random watermark positions. They are as common as booklets with all watermarks uniformly upright, or inverted.

Booklets may be broken down or exploded into separate sheets. Everything is then mounted, panes of stamps, covers, interleaving. When broken down in this way, they must be carefully unstitched, to preserve the binding strip of each pane. Some collectors say that this is changing the form of issue, almost mutilating the booklet, to be compared with soaking off the gum of a stamp. No longer as issued, the booklet could be a less desirable item when the time comes to sell. A compromise, for those who can afford it, is to have two of everything, one intact, one exploded for display. Appealing as this solution appears, it requires second thoughts when a single booklet may cost pounds.

Booklets contain the most commonly used denominations. In the past this has meant that there must be sufficient versatility to cover prepayment of basic inland letter, postcard and printed paper rates, with the emphasis on the first of these. Today booklets should accommodate basic second- and first-class mail charges. When postage rates change, adjustments to content must follow, and this alone explains most of the format variations over the years. An added attraction of booklets is that they contain printed extracts of principal postage rates, at home and abroad, within their covers.

The $1\frac{1}{2}$d and $2\frac{1}{2}$d were already in use when they first made their debut in Queen Elizabeth booklets. At first the King George VI 2s 6d and 5s editions continued, but from May 1953 the $1\frac{1}{2}$d and $2\frac{1}{2}$d panes were replaced with the normal Wilding definitives. For the time being the old 1d and $\frac{1}{2}$d panes in both booklets, and the 2d in the 5s version, remained. These were replaced by Queen Elizabeth issues from March 1954. A new denomination, 3s 9d, containing three panes of six $2\frac{1}{2}$d values, was the first all-new-reign booklet, introduced to meet the demands from the public who wanted only stamps for letters.

First printings of the $1\frac{1}{2}$d were in a distinct bluish-green

13. OLD-STYLE BOOKLETS
Left-hand row shows typical covers as they appeared in the mid 1950s. Later the covers were streamlined and given a more modern look

14. PICTORIAL BOOKLETS

Typical of the early booklet covers, placed on sale for a limited
period, after the Post Office went pictorial. In the bottom row the
10s booklet with Scott lasted only one edition. It is the only source
for the 1d plus 4d sepia pane. The 5s booklet arranged specially
for the 1970 International Exhibition, containing only stamp-dealers
advertisements

shade, but later they reverted to the normal sheet colour. Apart from inverted watermarks, which by now existed on all values between ½d and 2½d, the 1d pane was collectable in its own right. One pane each of the ½d, 1½d and 2½d totals 2s 3d. Rather than add an extra ½d pane, it was decided to include three 1d stamps. Three spaces remained, and were of course watermarked, and these were printed as a security measure. Initially each label carried the same message 'Please post early in the day', but later this was changed to three separate requests: 'Pack your parcels securely', 'Address your letters correctly' and 'Post early in the day'. They are to be found with Tudor watermark upright or inverted.

In an era of austerity, only from September 1953 was part-interleaving introduced. Pages interposed between all stamp panes had to wait until January 1955.

Towards the end of 1955, the St Edward watermark stamps made its intermittent appearance in booklets. For some months they were issued with mixed panes, some watermarks old, some new. Even the 3s 9d with only one value stamp exists with different watermarks on successive panes, within the same booklet.

Composition changes continually took place. First from January 1957, the 5s booklet adopted the lighter 2d, in place of the red-brown. On 1 June 1956 printed papers went up to 2d, so ending the useful life of the 1½d stamp. It was not until April 1957 that the booklets recognised this, with a recasting of 2s 6d contents to a single pane each of 2½d, 2d and ½d. The advertisement pane of 1d stamps disappeared. Later when letters cost 3d, and postcards 2½d, the 3s 9d booklet was replaced by a 4s 6d version with 18 3d stamps, and in January 1958 the other prices were also revised. New contents of the 5s consisted of two panes of 3d, and one pane each of 2½d, 1d and ½d, while the 2s 6d was converted to a 3s edition. This contained one pane each of 3d, 1½d, 1d and ½d, these low values providing sufficient variety for all domestic rates.

A second round of mixed booklets began towards the end of 1958 with the watermark switch to multiple crown without cypher. The earliest edition known is July 1958, and only this one and the 3s exist with both watermarks.

A tranquil period followed; only the covers were changed.

Originally with circular GPO cypher, this was replaced by an oval version in January 1955. Complete restyling in January 1959 was followed in December 1960 with a larger GPO cypher.

An experimental booklet costing 10s was placed on sale in April 1961. Only two editions were sold with the format of five 3d, and single 2d, 1½d, 1d and ½d panes, totalling 1,385,400 copies. From April it was recast with 2d and ½d panes giving way to one at 2½d, and seven editions of around half a million each were sold in the next few years.

With multiple crown watermark inverted, the 2d is one of the scarcer modern Great Britain low-value definitives. Theoretically about four million could exist, but most were used on ordinary correspondence and then lost. Even those salvaged by collectors are often imperfect, because the knife-edge separation is invariably slightly off true. One or more sides end up with straight edges or clipped perforations, making them worth less than perfect copies. Issued in 1961 and on sale for nearly a year all over the country, these 2d stamps were sought after by dealers at £3.50, and offered at £5 in 1970, an appreciation of over 60,000 per cent. These panes were not specially prepared: out of store came the cylinders last used in 1957.

In May 1965 the internal letter post was raised to 4d, and postcards cost 3d. All booklets changed again. Between June and August the 3s was repriced 4s 6d with two 4d and one 1d panes, the single denomination 4s 6d became 6s with three 4d panes, and the 10s continued with four at 4d, and single 3d and 1d panes. The 5s booklet was withdrawn in August 1965.

Meanwhile the phosphor and graphite experiments had been taking place in Southampton. Graphite-lined stamps appeared in booklets from July 1959, and all three regular editions, 3s, 4s 6d and 5s, were printed for use in Southampton. Although the normal ½d, 1d and 1½d sheet stamps exist only with St Edward's watermark, these booklet stamps were printed on multiple crown paper throughout, as were some of the ½d and 1d coils. All values from ½d to 3d, with the exception of the 2d, exist with watermark inverted, for these booklets were produced in the usual way. The only source of the 1½d crown graphite is from booklets; less than a million inverted watermark copies were printed, and their comparative rarity is recognised by the catalogues. Even scarcer is the 2½d with inverted watermark: it appeared only in 5s booklets. A residual printing of this value was prepared to use up the remaining stocks of graphite-lined paper after the experiment was abandoned, and widely distributed outside the Southampton area. Most of these stamps were lost to collectors.

Booklets were reissued with the phosphor line treatment, and although many do not recognise, or bother to differentiate between the various types of coating, there are nevertheless some highly sought after variations. Initially with green phosphor, they were almost immediately replaced with the second, blue version. 39,600 5s green booklets were issued in which the 2½d stamps were treated with two lines. Later editions show the revised one line version. Only 600,000 2½d stamps with two phosphor lines and watermark inverted were issued, and far, far less have survived. Readily selling at £10, this must hold the record for quick appreciation—nearly 100,000 per cent in ten years. Not that many collectors or dealers have made their fortune. It fetches such high prices because only a handful survived. Few had the foresight to lay in stocks while it was current. Even the one band version is not common, with only a million booklets containing this stamp in over three years.

Coinciding with the 4d post, new versions duly appeared with phosphor, and from 1967 all booklets were treated. From September 1967 until May 1968 only 6s booklets contained Machin Head stamps, with three panes of 4ds. In May 1968 there was one edition of the 4s 6d before a radically new policy was initiated by the Post Office. With one eye on the collector and the other on the housewife, they launched pictorial covers. Proofs were widely distributed to the press of the three themes. Ships on 4s 6d, birds for the 6s and explorers featured on 10s editions. Planned to change every few months, they were joined by a 5s booklet containing only 5d stamps, showing Stately Homes as the cover theme, in late 1968.

Last but not least in 1969, a large-size 15-stamp pane booklet selling at £1. One pane of 5d, two at 4d, and a fourth with varied values se-tenant showing three rows of 4d + 1d + 5d + 1d + 4d. In addition the interleaves and pane stubs are filled with recipes. Cheese platter salad or baked stuffed haddock, and ten more tempting tasty dishes are all included for the pound, and unlike most books when you have used up the stamps, the menus remain. Handy wallet and handbag size, it may well be the shape of things to come.

Booklets sold from slot machines were introduced on an experimental basis in 1936. In 1952 two different types were still in use, officially types D and E. They continued into the Elizabethan age with new reign stamps. Type D was made up of ½d, 1d and 1½d values in panes of two, inside plain white covers, all watermark upright. Type E had the same contents but in panes of four. Both Tudor and St Edward's watermarks were used, and although the D type was discontinued in November 1960, the E variety lasted until the end of 1964. During the last five years multiple crown watermark has been used in the E type, and all versions in this booklet exist normal or inverted.

On 22 April 1959 the now familiar 2s booklet was placed on sale at selected offices, and over the years the number of machines was extended to cover most large offices. ½d, 1d, 1½d and 3d stamps on St Edward's upright or inverted paper were included in the prototype, known as the bacon booklet, because all the printed interleaves advertised the merits of this breakfast food. Only one printing was made. Then the booklet reappeared with multiple crown watermark. After two editions, the Post Office, convinced that this slot-machine version had come to stay, invited the printers to set up a new cylinder. Apparently unchanged, the layout of the stamps on the plate was sideways, producing further watermark positions. The head to tail arrangement used in the counter booklets continued for these, so that stamps exist with the watermark facing to the right or to the left, when viewed from the back of the stamp. As at that time some coil stamps already existed with watermark sideways to the right, the left-facing version is normally called 'reversed'.

An innovation in July 1963, a special holiday edition, still valued at 2s, was placed on sale at selected resorts. It contained nine 2½d stamps for use on postcards, and three ½d stamps to make up the 2s value. Two panes of four 2½d stamps were of normal appearance, but one pane was made up of the odd 2½d and three ½d values, se-tenant. This novelty value gave the sales a boost, but in fact both stamps are quite distinct. Printed on

15. SHIP BOOKLETS
A range of the popular 4s 6d covers. Each ship design was on sale
for two to three months before replacement

16. WILDING SE-TENANT

Early pane showing three spare labels used for Post Office publicity.
Two panes from Holiday Booklets, to accommodate 2½d stamps for
postcards. After the 4d letter rate, the 3d + 1d pane was included
in all slot-machine booklets

a heavy quality chalk paper, they are readily distinguishable. Some recognise as a variety a last minute reprint in September 1963, with binding thread white in place of black.

Pleased with the results, the Post Office decided to reissue the booklet the following year with some modifications. Now consisting of four panes, each made up of two 2½d and two ½d stamps se-tenant, these too are distinguishable. Although sideways watermarked, the 2½d is type 2 with the redrawn tiara. This 1964 edition was reissued at Christmas, although strangely only at those selfsame resorts. One would have thought that most of them would have been deserted in the grey November days! A final holiday booklet, first issued at Christmas 1965, with two panes of 3d stamps, reflected the increase in the cost of living.

From June 1965 the regular issues appeared with se-tenant values, one pane of 4d joined by one pane with pairs of 1d and 3d. Two-value panes present few problems. To the printer it is purely a two-colour job, each value in turn receiving its impression on the multicolour press.

Phosphor lines left their mark on the series. While a postage rise can be dealt with by revising contents, it also means a rearrangement of the overprinted lines. When the switch to 4d and 1d + 3d took place, the phosphor 3d stamps had one line placed at the left or the right as an overlap of the 1d line. Later all stamps were printed with two lines.

New Machin Head definitives did not interfere with contents, which remained unchanged until the 3d post ceased. Then 4d stamps only were included, one complete pane, and one with two stamps and an advertisement attached.

Coils or rolls of stamps have been issued by the Post Office in bewildering variety. Apart from the well-known versions that disgorge as pennies are fed into the slot, a wide range was made up for commercial users. Sophisticated machinery can fold circulars or letters, insert them into envelopes, then seal them, and finally add the stamp. Coils are sold with three different-sized central cores, in various lengths, and delivery can be arranged sideways, or vertically, according to the nature of the machine.

Some coils are printed from a special cylinder, with 21 rows instead of 20, so giving a continuous impression on the web of the paper. They are later sliced into vertical strips, and assembled in the required roll length. Some sizes and denominations are not demanded in quantities sufficiently large to justify the expenses of a special cylinder. They are made up from normal sheets, in strips, and then gummed together. These joins are collected.

Finally there are the sideways watermarked varieties. Certain coils in horizontal formation enjoy continuous demand. When the paper was watermarked, the layout of the impressions on the roll was sideways. These watermark varieties were never easy to find, for they were rarely on sale at post offices. Dealers had to buy complete rolls, and most collectors did not bother to keep up to date. There seems to be a built-in antipathy to paying more than face value for current stamps!

Watermark sideways varieties include: Tudor, $1\frac{1}{2}$d, 2d and $2\frac{1}{2}$d; St Edward, $1\frac{1}{2}$d to 3d inclusive; Crown, 2d to 4d inclusive; Phosphor, 2d, 3d and 4d; all these are from rolls.

A curious variety sometimes occurs, known as the coil jump. As the printing continues along the web, the perforating comb is readjusted, giving the appearance of a stagger on adjacent pair. If the machine is slipping, this may be as large as one or two millimetres. They are not hard to find, but they are unusual.

Latest in the coil-dispensing experiments is the Machin Head se-tenant roll, already referred to. It is quite possible that this will replace the now familiar 2s booklet.

Rolls of stamps cannot be collected in the normal way. It would be both impracticable and unwise, expense apart, to store one coil of everything. An acceptable solution is to mount the leader, and the first six stamps attached to it. The coil leader has printed on it the Post Office stock code, contents, total cost, and other technical information. With only one such leader to a roll, one either buys the complete coil, and use the remaining stamps on letters, or purchase from a dealer at an understandable premium. More modestly, one has to be content with a pair or strip of four. If it shows a coil join, or coil jump, so much the better, but these are not always to be found to order.

Whatever the future, it would seem that coils will always be with us. A Philatelic Bureau circular listed 48 distinct rolls in early 1970, but rationalisation has meant that the number of types stocked is now severely curtailed. An up-to-date list of rolls available may be seen in the current *Post Office Guide,* or can be obtained from the Philatelic Bureau.

9

Postal Stationery

Ignored for so many years, postal stationery is slowly creeping back into favour. Back in Queen Victoria's time, everyone collected it, but when Stanley Gibbons decided to discontinue listings in their catalogue, this facet was killed stone dead. Like sheep, all but a few turned away and concentrated on the adhesive issues. It was left to a few to keep the torch alight, and much of the information lies forgotten in unknown archives.

In the British philatelic press there was, from time to time, the odd news item on stationery. It was of necessity quite vague, often based on an official press release. Varieties in make-up were rarely chronicled, and even new denominations or styles were reported only as a matter of chance.

This state of affairs continued well into the present reign, so that even now complete collections of Great Britain Queen Elizabeth post office stationery are scarce. But a start has been made. *The Woodstock Catalogue of British Elizabethan Stamps* made up its first simplified listing in the 1970 edition, and slowly but surely the story of the past years is being told.

Stationery is issued to prepay basic postage rates, and in Great Britain the current range includes postcards, reply cards, letter cards, envelopes, registered envelopes, and aerogrammes. Other items such as newspaper wrappers are to be found from time to time, but these are privately printed and prepared. The complete list of official issues is in theory available over the counter of any Post Office. In practice the situation is rather different.

Take an ordinary item like the common postcard. Four de-

17. MACHIN SE-TENANT

First se-tenant pane from a 10s booklet, with pane badly trimmed, making bottom row imperforate, thus detracting from its collector value. Two panes from 2s slot-machine booklets. After the two-tier post, all slot-machine booklets contained six stamps. Advertising on the two spare labels

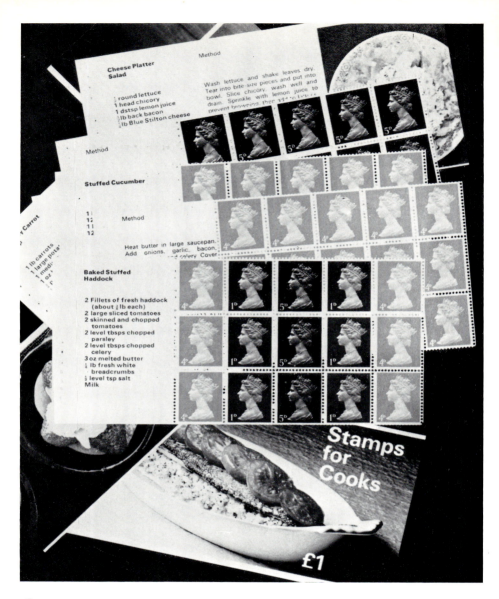

18. THE COOK BOOKLET
Sold at £1 in Southern England only, they were in demand for the
multiple value pane

nominations have been issued, and a simplified listing is short enough. A new side-face portrait of the Queen, within a simple border, with the figures of value placed in the top right corner, and the inscription 'Postage' along the base, was released in 1955. Typographed, a letterpress process, by McCorquodale and Co. Ltd, in dark brown and valued at 2d, it formed the franking portion of a buff postcard. This was inscribed 'Post Card', these words flanking the Garter Arms. Later issues were on creamier paper before the change to 2½d carmine, following on the 1957 postage increases. This last item is scarce, for every succeeding 2½d printing incorporated the Royal Coat-of-Arms.

In due course they were replaced by 3d violet cards, part of the 1965 revision. The Post Office began to revise their stationery in 1968, prior to becoming a public corporation. For the postcards this meant farewell to the Royal Arms, leaving just the simple description 'Post Card'. They also took the opportunity to change the colour of the card to pale blue. A further example was released to coincide with the two-tier postage system on 16 September 1968. A new printed stamp, 4d sepia, adopted the Machin Head, flanked on each side by the word 'Postage', and the value in figures set below the portrait. Fine as the head may be in photogravure, it was disappointing on the cards. Letterpress cannot convey the delicate tones and shadows as conceived by the artist and interpreted by the photographer.

In 1969 a quick check around the post offices in many parts of the country produced a variety of cards on sale. The last three versions, 3d on cream, 3d on pale blue, and 4d sepia were all available, although never more than one type at any single office. Requests were usually countered with the same stock response, 'No-one ever asks for these any more'. The days of a short cheap message have passed away for ever.

Complementing the postcards are the relatively unknown reply cards. These were issued under international regulations, consisting of two cards printed together, both ready stamped and folded in two. One card is intended for the outward message and the second card may then be detached and used for the reply.

Although bearing a British stamp they could be posted abroad, to prepay a message back to Great Britain. Any necessary extra postage was also prepaid by British adhesive stamps. Little used, very few offices stocked them, although they could be obtained to order. They are inscribed 'Post Card with reply paid', and 'The annexed card is intended for answer', on the forward half with the equivalent French instructions. The reply half bears in English and French 'Post-Card Reply', and 'This half is only available for transmission to Great Britain', and in English only 'Great Britain'. All cards carry the Garter Arms.

The first issue, 2d + 2d brown, was placed on sale in 1955, initially on buff and later on cream card. In 1958 they became 2½d + 2½d carmine on white, and there are variations in the settings of the instructions for use. A 3d + 3d violet on white card version issued in 1965 was followed by a short-lived violet on pale blue. Tariff revisions of 1968 brought forth a 4d + 4d sepia Machin Head printing, also with a limited life, soon replaced with stamp and words in red, conforming to the adhesive stamp colour changes. Considering the almost negligible use, these three printings in as many years must become comparatively difficult to find unless stocks have been put on one side. In commercially used condition they are almost impossible to secure.

A popular item in the suite of stationery is the familiar letter-card. They combine the convenience of envelope and paper, with the secrecy of an ordinary letter. They can accommodate small items such as photographs or coupons, and are ideal for that urgent message. In the same style as the postcards with Garter Arms, the first Elizabethan letter-card was issued with a 2½d stamp. Appearing in 1955 it was not replaced until 1957 with a similar 3d version. Initially on cream card, and then on white, it too was later printed with the Royal Coat-of-Arms. During its long life a number of printing changes affected the settings of the instructions and the provision for a senders address. In 1965 a 4d pale blue version was quickly supplanted by a simple 'Letter Card' version, without arms, in 1968.

A choice of two rates in 1968 caused the Post Office to add a 5d deep blue Machin Head version in their list, but for some months the 4d blue continued side by side with the 5d. There was some excitement at the National Stamp Exhibition in 1969: a few letter-cards printed with a 4d sepia Machin Head stamp were found in the temporary automatic sales suite attached to the special post office. Once exhausted, no more were placed on sale, and no official explanation was forthcoming. Then, as collectors were becoming resigned to the situation, a new stationery list issued by the Philatelic Bureau was found to contain three separate types of 4d Machin Head letter-cards. They offered 4d sepia, 4d sepia with one phosphor line, and the 4d red also with one line, simultaneously. It was fortunate for collectors that the Bureau had extended their service to include stationery, for every post office I called at in January 1970 seemed still to stock only the obsolete 4d blue.

The Post Office admitted in 1970 that the quality of reproduction of the stamp design on postcards and letter-cards was below standard. Accordingly they decided to print the stamp on these cards by photogravure, and the first in this improved style was the 5d blue. It was placed on sale at the Philatelic Bureau, and at the philatelic counters from 20 April 1970.

Envelopes sold by the Post Office bore no message or instructions at first. The stamp, a bas-relief portrait of the Queen by Cecil Thomas, within a circle flanked by 'Value Postage Value', is embossed. Overall the stamp is in the shape of a Tudor rose. On rare occasions the embossed stamp appears albino, when the colour has failed to print through lack of ink.

Over the years the sizes of envelopes have varied. The first of the reign appeared in Size A, 120 × 93mm, and B, 136 × 79mm, Both were issued in 1954 with 2½d red embossed stamp, on cream stock, but shortly afterwards the A envelope was changed to grey-blue.

Inevitably changes followed postage increases, and both sizes were reissued with 3d purple values. The small format of the B envelope was not popular, and it was increased to 162 × 114mm, still on creamy paper. Further changes in June 1965 saw both envelopes with a 4d blue embossed stamp.

As part of the standardisation programme, the Post Office issued POP (Post Office Preferred) sizes during the course of 1968. A printed message and dotted lines for the sender's address appeared on the reverse flap. New sizes, A 146 × 95mm and B 235 × 120mm, were far more sensible, the smaller adequate for the usual personal letter, and the larger versatile enough for most enclosures. It was planned that POP envelopes would attract ordinary postage rates, and that non-standard sizes would cost more, but this was at first deferred after a long and costly campaign.

Both sizes of envelopes were available for either second- or first-class mail. Pending new embossed dies, 4d envelopes carried a 4d stamp, and an additional double ring reading 'Postage 1d extra', placed at the left. All stamps and the rings were in sepia. Another first, the 4d + 1d envelopes, came with two phosphor lines, and later some of the 4d envelopes carried one line, always clear of the embossed stamp. The paper for this new series was a glossy blue-grey.

Later printings in 1969 were in revised colours, conforming with adhesive stamps. They became 4d red, and 4d + 1d blue.

Towards the end of 1969 the long-awaited new embossed die was introduced, adapting the Machin Head. Tastefully constructed in the form of an octagon, the value is placed beneath the head with 'postage' flanking left and right. First on the scene was the size 'A' 5d blue, in all other respects identical with the interim 4d + 1d blue, which had itself enjoyed the now familiar short life.

Registered envelopes could easily fill a chapter by themselves. There are so many, three or four sizes of every issue, and it only requires a postage or a registration fee rise for new versions to be issued. This account is sufficient for the simplified collector. Dyed-in-the-wool specialists examine every setting of the printed instructions, and measure the cut of the paper, and even look at the printer's imprint, usually hidden away under the gummed flap.

Unused examples of the early envelopes are scarce, as once again few collectors or dealers bothered to put any to one side. Those that did were content, only too often, to secure just one example, and the largest sizes are hard to find in nice mint condition. Too unwieldy for the normal album page, they were rejected. Used copies are easier to locate, as there are still a number of collectors who never throw anything philatelic away, and they reappear in auctions, ensuring a continuing source of supply.

The Queen Elizabeth series show just how the value of money has changed, as the service costs more and more. Registration guarantees not only compensation in respect of loss, but also a signature from every postal officer en route to destination.

19. STATIONERY DIES

(*top*) Tudor Rose design for envelopes (*centre*) Tudor Rose adapted for registration envelopes (*bottom*) Stationery Die for postcards, reply cards and lettercards

20. STATIONERY—the first fifteen years
Reply cards 2½d and 3d; lettercard 4d; envelope 3d; registration
envelope 3s, used by forces post offices abroad

Personal handling of this kind becomes more and more expensive to provide.

At first four envelopes were placed on sale in 1954. Sizes, with official Post Office designations were F 132 × 84mm, G 155 × 95mm, H 233 × 120mm and K 288 × 150mm. All envelopes were inscribed 'Registered Letter' and bore an embossed grey stamp in the Tudor Rose design reading 'Registration sixpence Postage twopence halfpenny 8½'. The 6d additional fee covered loss or damage to an inland letter up to £5, and the entire loss of a registered letter to a place abroad up to £2 18s. Extra cover, inland, could be obtained on prepayment of an additional fee. For valuable articles abroad registration has never been the appropriate means of safeguard. An insured letter service is provided in its place.

In 1956 the inland registration fee was raised to one shilling, and for the first and only time a differential charge was made for overseas. This remained at 6d, recognising the comparatively small cover offered. Two series of envelopes were placed on sale, side by side, at British post offices. In place of the old heading they were entitled 'Inland Registered Letter' and 'Overseas Registered Letter' respectively.

Inland registered letters were at first issued with the same 8½d embossed stamp, and an additional double ring in blue reading 'Minimum Registration 6d Extra'. Usually when such provisionals are used it is a temporary arrangement while newly valued embossed dies are prepared. Eventually, from around August 1957, the 1s 2½d envelopes did appear, the die revised to read 'Registration and Postage', the actual division between the two elements no longer specifically noted. Entire loss within the inland service was now covered up to £10.

In October increases in letter postage rates brought yet more envelopes, at 1s 3d, although they did not reach the counters until August 1959. The concessionary rate for overseas mail was abolished, and the heading reverted to 'Registered Letter'.

Now inflation gathered momentum. In February 1961 registration was raised to 1s 6d, and 1s 9d envelopes followed on sale. This higher fee covered loss up to £20, but was itself soon supplanted by a further rise in 1963 to 1s 9d. At first there were provisional envelopes again, 1s 9d + 3d, to be replaced in turn by definitives in 1964.

In turn, postage went up and the combined fee of 1s 9d registration and 4d postage was satisfied by envelopes with a 2s 1d stamp from June 1965. This was the last series of the small-size F envelopes. The F size had steadily lost ground to the larger G size, especially since both cost the same.

A reassessment of Post Office revenues showed that the registration service was losing money fast. The high handling content made it uneconomical, and in 1966 the fee was raised to 3s, covering loss or damage up to £100. The familiar pattern was repeated with provisionals 2s 1d + 1s 3d on sale from October 1966, to be followed in June 1967 with 3s 4d definitives.

International agreements concluded with the Universal Postal Union brought forth the next change—a new heading reading 'Registered Letter—Recommandé'. This was coupled with a change in the size of the largest K envelope to 232 × 120mm. Discontent and muttering in commercial circles over this sudden decrease in format was coupled with an equally drastic decline in sales. For once the Post Office reconsidered its policy, and the 1967 envelope was restyled to an extra large 305 × 153mm format on a temporary basis, to be replaced in its turn by the old 288 × 150mm size.

No choice was offered to users of the registration system, when two tiers were introduced. It all had to travel first class. So again the Post Office issued provisionals, 3s 4d + 1d, a blue circle containing the wording 'Minimum Extra Postage 1d'. On 13 April 1970 the new octagonal design was placed on sale for all three 3s 5d grey envelopes.

The overseas mail series of 1955 was issued with a 6d maroon embossed stamp simply reading 'sixpence registration sixpence'. Only two sizes were on sale G2 and K2, identical with the G and K inland formats. In 1957 they were revalued at 6d + 6d. Later these envelopes were replaced by 1s blue stamped editions, but these were not available within the British Isles. Their heading gives the clue. Reading 'Forces Overseas Registered Letter', they were printed solely for use at Forces Post Offices abroad. Forces are entitled to concessional postage rates: in western Europe, for instance, mail prepaid at the normal inland letter rates went by air, and if sea mail was considered sufficiently speedy then even lower rates were charged. A registered letter within the Forces Post Office system in western

Germany, or by sea mail to the United Kingdom, in 1956 cost only 7½d, 6d registration and 1½d postage. There was a small continuing demand for such concessional rates, and, in addition, on active service it may happen that the postage element is remitted altogether, but registration still must be paid for. As a compromise, forces envelopes are embossed with the registration element only, and postage is added by adhesive stamps. So the anomaly remains, that British Post Office registered envelopes, ordered and supplied by them, are not on sale anywhere within the British Isles, but they are available in any part of the world where there are sufficient troops of any of the fighting arms, to justify a post office or postal detachment.

The 1s envelopes were in due course replaced by 1s 6d, 1s 6d + 3d, 1s 9d and 3s envelopes, but only in size G2. In 1968 these envelopes were reissued with Reccomandé heading.

Aerogrammes, or airletters as they were once called, have received far more attention than any other items of stationery. In part this must be due to the publicity mounted by the Post Office and their continued use as a vehicle for special and commemorative issues. Another factor is their strong appeal to airmail collectors, a well-organised international band. There are no official airmail stamps issued in Great Britain, and airletters are a satisfactory substitute. But it is still surprising that this inconveniently-sized, flimsy-papered stationery should have gained pre-eminence at the expense of cards or envelopes.

Specialists recognise many sub-types and variations. The cut of the form, the spacing of the letterpress, and the fineness of the screen used in printing the stamp, offer scope for study. For these variations a good handbook or specialised catalogue is essential. As an introduction there is sufficient material in the basic issues themselves.

Airletters are printed on light-weight paper. Originally designed to be folded into four and then sealed by a gummed flap, they provided, and still provide, a cheap method of sending a message by air abroad. They are so light that the Post Office can afford a substantial discount on regular air fees. One drawback is that no enclosures are permitted, but as the system depends upon the light, almost featherweight nature of the forms, this is hardly surprising.

M. C. Farrar-Bell's design for the 1s 6d Coronation commemorative was adapted by changing the wording and value to make a 6d carmine stamp. This was printed in photogravure on the form, and letterpress additions of the ER cypher, emblems and caption. This produced the second commemorative Great Britain airletter. The first had been issued some five years earlier for the Wembley Olympic Games. These apart, the impressed stamp had always been normal size, but all Queen Elizabeth issues bear double-size designs.

The Coronation airletter was placed on sale at the same time as the four postage stamps, 3 June 1953. It remained on sale for some months, before the first definitive airletter of the reign, issued 1 January 1954. This had an impressed stamp identical to the Coronation issue, except that the date was replaced by the value. It remained on sale for four years.

A second commemorative issue was made for the 46th Parliamentary Conference. Already almost ignored by a single small format 4d adhesive, this event was surprisingly selected for a special airletter. A new design featuring the Houses of Parliament, and the clock tower which houses Big Ben, was unusually pictorial. Printed by photogravure, it was overprinted by letterpress in blue, simply naming the meeting. Issued on 12 September 1957 it remained on sale for one month. It was replaced on 14 October 1957 by the same form without overprint, as a definitive issue. This coincidence, and the temporary nature of the overprint, raised speculation that the new form had been designed, and was on the point of issue, when last-minute rescheduling provided a simple commemorative, before the new definitives were placed in circulation.

Nine years later the stamp was still going strong, although in the intervening years the composition of the form had been changed. At first the address quarter was located in the top right, but business interests suggested that the lower right would be more suitable, especially for typists. An experimental printing confirmed these views, and all succeeding printings were so arranged.

The increase in rates to 9d meant a change of value, but not in design. Instead on 3 October 1966, it was eventually replaced on 1 July 1968.

Meanwhile the Post Office was making comparatively daring innovations. In the London area two pictorial airletters were

21. STATIONERY—the new look

Two-tier postage produced a number of new items. Reply card, and lettercard with the Machin Head adaption. The 4d envelope, and its modification for first class 5d mail

The Tower and Tower Bridge. London   Photograph by courtesy of the British Travel & Holiday Association

Houses of Parliament from the Embankment. London   Photograph by courtesy of the British Travel & Holiday Association

22. PICTORIAL AIRLETTERS
An early Post Office experiment, on sale in London only, and
intended for tourist use. Sales were disappointing and the idea
discontinued

placed on sale, showing respectively the Houses of Parliament from across the River Thames, and The Tower of London from Tower Bridge. They carried the usual 6d stamp, and the views were in three superimposed colours, producing the full range of the spectrum.

Issued on 1 August 1963, they were allowed to circulate for a complete season before withdrawal on 31 March the following year. Half a million of each design were printed and the forms were sold at 1od each. The experiment was deemed unsuccessful, and this particular idea was not repeated. Despite publicity, they were not widely bought, and the unsold forms could be seen to get grubbier and dog-eared, as they lingered behind the counter.

Undeterred, two commemorative airletters were issued for the Shakespeare Festival bearing a special stamp. One of the forms shows six scenes from Shakespeare's plays, and the other the theatre at Stratford-upon-Avon, Warwickshire. This later photograph was wrongly described as the 'Shakespeare Memorial Theatre' on the first million printed, and was then corrected to 'Royal Shakespeare Theatre'. One million of the revised version were printed, but of the combined total about one million were unsold, and destroyed. The play-scenes form also sold about one million copies. These forms cost 1od each, fourpence more than their value for postage.

A new definitive aerogramme was released on 1 July 1968, and again the designer was David Gentleman. The stamp, an outline of a VC-10 airliner in blue and white, appears on this revised format form, arranged to be folded into three. This permits the complete sealing of contents, and conformed to new international requirements. Numerous reprintings show variations in colour from pale to light blue.

The new stamp was adapted for the commemorative aerogramme placed on sale as part of the set in honour of the Investiture of the Prince of Wales. With address section cachet, and a pictorial view of the castle at Caernarvon, it is the first bilingual British aerogramme, with additional inscriptions in Welsh.

From 1965 the Post Office issued an annual series of Christmas airletters and aerogrammes. Like all the special forms they were sold at 1od each, although at first the postage element was only 6d. Later issues prepay 9d postage, making the pictorial form, at one penny, a very cheap form of Christmas greeting.

Two forms were issued on 1 November 1965. One had a predominantly religious theme, with nativity scene. The lithographed stamp, with its Wilding portrait in purple, shows a snowflake pattern on red background. The other form is made up of seven different snowflake designs, with a blue portrait of the Queen, and yet another snowflake on a blue background for the stamp. For some unexplained reason they were not withdrawn until 31 December, over a week after the last practicable day of use.

In 1966 another form was released on 1 November, this time with the year on the front panel. The stamp, now 9d, portrays a Christmas Rose, pine cone, and cameo portrait of the Queen. The pictorial section features Father Christmas, flying between Christmas trees, with his loaded sledge in the snow-covered foreground.

Two forms were issued on 1 November 1967. A nativity scene with the Three Wise Men appears on one, and a partridge in a pear tree on the other. Both have the same stamp, Christmas candles on a green background. Only the pear-tree form bears the date.

In 1968 there were again two forms. Father Christmas is in an airship, looking through his telescope, and the front cachet shows him firing a cannon with the repeated date 25 Dec 1968 as ammunition. Christmas trees on a red background form the main feature of the stamp. An angel playing a trumpet is the central motif of the other form, with choirboy cachet, and the Star of Bethlehem on a blue background is used in the stamp design.

An earlier start was made in 1969. One form, created by Fritz Wegner, the designer of the contemporary adhesive stamps, continued the style he had established there. Mary and Joseph are seen journeying to Bethlehem on the stamp and other nativity scenes are shown on the front and central panels.

One exception from this record of issued stationery items is the Christmas card that might have been. In June 1966 it was announced that the Post Office was preparing their own card for sale to the public. It would depict an early post office scene printed upside down in relation to the stamp, which it was intended should show some modern aspect of the Post Office, such as the Post Office Tower. On receipt the card could be folded to show the picture side only, and it could then be displayed like any other. Political or commercial motives must have intervened, for this card, assured of success, never appeared.

Any chronicle of postal stationery would not be complete without some mention of privately arranged, stamped-to-order items. Post Office stationery is sold at the cost of the stamp with a little extra for the card or envelope. Regular aerogrammes are sold at the price of postage alone.

For business firms, or indeed any other user, there are arrangements to stamp unfolded envelopes or cards with any desired amount of stamps. This facility has occasionally been used by stamp clubs and exhibitions, more often by philatelists and dealers intent on securing examples of awkward values, and most frequently by commercial houses. Typical examples are large envelopes containing company reports, stamped cards for proxy voting, and newspaper wrappers. This last section is particularly fruitful, thanks to a large wholesale newsagent, W. H. Smith and Son Ltd.

Today examples are less likely to be found, for a charge is made for stamping, in addition to the cost of the stamps themselves. But they still appear, and are just as much postage stamps as those appearing on the official issues. Since they may be ordered at will, philatelically inspired examples are less desirable than commercial specimens.

Postcards, wrappers and labels are surface-printed by the Stationery Office press at Harrow, and envelopes (unfolded) are embossed by the Inland Revenue at London, Manchester and Edinburgh. Charges vary, averaging £1 per thousand, with a minimum of 1,000 charged, no matter how few are required. This makes it difficult for the philatelist to add varieties to his collection inexpensively, and also explains the high prices charged by dealers, as there is but a limited market for such oddities. Commercially used items, on the other hand, are just as desirable, and far harder to track down than the regular Post Office issues.

Like any other form of printing, errors creep in from time to time. Embossed stamps miss their colour, and perhaps the embossing die strikes twice. Sometimes the embossing misses altogether, and only the letterpress printing remains to show that this is really an official item. Some of these errors escape from the printing works

One final stationery item is almost completely overlooked— the reply coupon. All that remains of the dream of one international postage stamp, these coupons are sold to cover postage back to Great Britain. They are exchangeable anywhere in the world, for stamps equivalent to the basic surface letter rate home. In addition to the international version, there is a Commonwealth Reply Coupon, sold at a reduced rate, that takes into account the lower tariffs between member nations. Little has been done towards listing these items, which naturally have appeared at a variety of prices over the inflationary years.

Stationery is experiencing a revival. Long neglected, more and more collectors realise that they form a proper part of any collection. Loose-leaf albums now take special leaves, which can house stationery, but the overriding problems have yet to be solved. The excessive bulk of even a modest collection remains the prime drawback.

23. CHRISTMAS AEROGRAMME
First Christmas Greetings Aerogramme, 1965. The specimen
overprint was used only on copies distributed for press purposes

24. EVOLUTION OF THE FIRST DAY COVER
Upper: Post Office official envelope and early large size handstamp, posted at Bladon, Oxford, where Sir Winston Churchill is buried.
Lower: An early commercial cover, and the original slogan postmark in use at selected offices

10

Post Office Services

Since the hobby began, a stamp collector has had to call in at a post office to buy the latest stamps. In 1953 no stocks of earlier issues were retained, no first-day envelopes provided, and for the tardy it was often a case of 'too late—all sold out'.

Today the picture is different. A service for collectors is offered, which may not provide everything, but goes a fair way towards that end.

At the beginning of the reign there were a few unpublicised facilities available. Stamps and postage-due labels, and certain of the overprinted Great Britain stamps for use in territories abroad, were obtainable by post. Not until 1 May 1963 was the Philatelic Bureau established. At first simple temporary offices were occupied in the Headquarters complex, hard by the London Chief Office. By post, or during certain hours on personal application, a range of stamps, ordinary and phosphor overprinted, current and recently obsolete, were on sale.

This was the first permanent selling organisation. For some years there had been temporary offices, as part of national and international stamp exhibitions, often crowded for room, although the spacious counter in the Festival Hall, for the London International Stamp Exhibition 1960, was a model of its kind.

Soon after the Bureau opened, the *Philatelic Bulletin* appeared. Very different from the luxury pocket-sized glossy with colour of today, that first issue in September 1963 consisted of 11 foolscap pages, and a supplement of special postmarks and handstamps, all in typewritten facsimile characters. It was a significant step forward; at last the collector could receive all the latest information on stamps, with helpful technical details for good measure. Following at roughly monthly intervals, the Bulletin brought philatelists up to date on many aspects of printing and production.

An additional bonus with issue No. 3, in November 1963, was a copy of the 1s 6d Compac commemorative, overprinted 'Cancelled' in red, as a substitute for an illustration. Copies treated in this way are now in demand. Other premiums for subscribers in those early days included a specimen of a Santa Claus letter to children, and the Reindeerland franking used with it, a Shakespeare airletter overprinted 'Cancelled', and examples of the test labels used in stamp machines. One of these was little known, prepared as part of the test programme for the early Post Office experiments in first-day cover servicing. Double-size, it was used in the machines that franked the Scout set automatically in 1957. These labels, grey for the small size, red for the larger version, read 'For testing purposes only'.

Beginning with Volume 3, a smaller format, printed bulletin was introduced, and apart from news on current and future sets, there were supporting features of more general interest. Probably one of the most revealing series depicts unaccepted designs for commemoratives. Everyone can become their own armchair critic, comparing the official choice with what might have been. Colour printing was used to great effect from 1968.

Although the principle of philatelic service had been established, complaints continued to be levelled at the slow service. Admitting shortcomings, it was explained officially that staff shortages, and the difficulties in recruiting the right type of assistance, were to blame. To overcome these problems, the Bureau moved to new premises in Edinburgh from October 1968. Unfortunately delays were still frequent, and it would seem that pressure on the staff, and the volume of orders, continues to rise.

The Post Office has issued a folder outlining the chief services of the Philatelic Bureau. In addition to details of their conditions for the sale of stamps, there is full information on their first-day cover service. With the exception of the Scout set, when an experimental scheme was tried out at Sutton Coldfield, all issues from the Coronation up to 1963 had to be posted privately, and received an ordinary postmark. A little help was offered from the Europa 1961 series, by selecting one office with a special postmark, and allowing philatelic mail to be handed in separately, to receive it.

In 1963 philatelic facilities became the rule. Freedom from Hunger sets could receive a special slogan postmark, although many covers were handed in at the National Stamp Exhibition, to be handstamped there after receiving a privately produced rubber cachet, applied in aid of the charity's funds. Starting with the Paris Conference 6d, a special slogan reading 'First Day of Issue' was used on all mail posted in 30 special boxes sited around the country. An applicant's own covers could be sent in, beginning with the Nature Week pair. The Bureau would, for a fee of 5½d, in addition to the cost of the stamps, affix the set, and arrange for special postmarking. These slogan marks, replacing the normal die, were carefully applied to all covers; the machines were run at a very reduced rate. Compac was not given the customary advance publicity, so for this last special stamp of the year, in addition to servicing private covers at 6d, they undertook to provide a plain envelope, address, stamp and post it for one shilling.

23 April 1964 taxed the philatelic services of the Post Office to the full. For the first time an official Post Office envelope was released to accompany the Shakespeare set. Not sold in unused condition, these covers were available to special order, with a complete set of stamps, posted at Stratford. So great was the demand that there was some delay in delivery, as the staff was overwhelmed. A new circular handstamp replaced the slogan die, and this has continued until the present day. Slogans are still used for bulk mailings, with minimum postings in the tens of thousands. In theory there is a continuing requirement for a complete set on cover to qualify for the first-day postmark, but this rule is not generally applied.

Subsequent issues often had their own covers, officially issued by the Post Office. These could be purchased at certain offices in advance, but it was not until 1965 that envelopes were made available as a matter of course.

Throughout the reign many commercial firms, and at one time the British Philatelic Association, arranged to manufacture special envelopes for collectors wishing to send a complete set with first-day postmark. These still continue with a selection to satisfy all tastes. Die-stamped, embossed, gold-leaf or plain printed, in colour or in black and white, they rival the official covers. An advantage not enjoyed by commercial organisations is an insight into the stamp designs. So with this advance information, the field is clear for the Post Office to arrange a designed cover, complementary to the set. As an added attraction they include a stiffener—a card which reduces damage to the envelope in transit—with informative technical and background data. Nevertheless commercial covers have their strong and faithful following, and this is likely to remain.

First-day covers have value. Why they are so sought after is difficult to pinpoint. The demand continues, and prices rise in sympathy. So much so, that they have already been forged. In one well-reported case, a non-existent headstamp reading 'Diss, Norfolk' was used. The instigator was traced, prosecuted and sentenced. Such forgeries are unlikely to be repeated.

Today three services are provided by the Bureau. Under Service A they provide the envelope, address it, add the stamps, cancel them with their own distinctive postmark, and despatch the finished article through the posts. Service B is similar, but the customer's own addressed envelope is used. More recently they have inaugurated Service C, for bulk orders of at least 50 envelopes of the same issue. It is similar to the A scheme, but addresses are added by mechanical means. Naturally a fee is charged for all these services, and they are much higher than those asked by some stamp dealers. Nevertheless thousands of covers are sent off every time a new set comes out.

Presentation packs are another innovation. A typical pack contains the 1968 Paintings series of four stamps, slipped into strips attached to a firm black card. This is supported by a printed colour folder, with full biographical details of the artists, with portraits. The 1967-68 low value Machin Heads pack includes a short history of the evolution of the accepted design, together with a pen portrait of the artist, and a brief description of the photogravure method of printing.

The first Post Office packs are relatively unknown. They were designed for use at a British Exhibition week in the USA, and priced in dollars and cents. Later they were placed on sale at the 1960 International Stamp Exhibition, held in the Festival Hall, London. Remaining stocks were available at later ex-

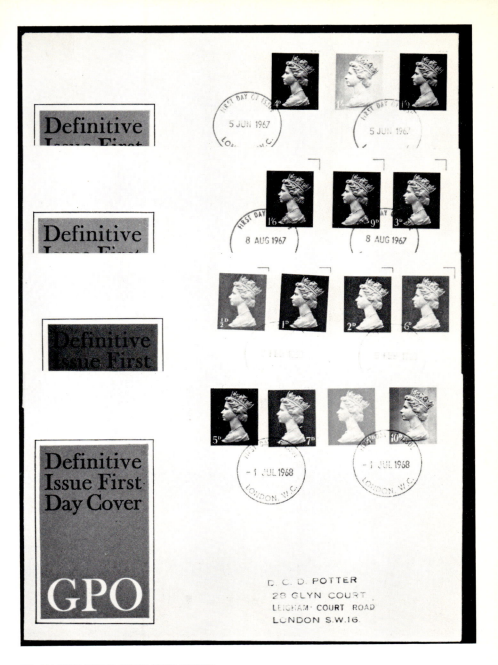

25. MACHIN HEAD FIRST DAY COVER
Original low-value definitives were issued in four instalments.
These covers show the smaller size handstamp, and the restrained
official first day covers

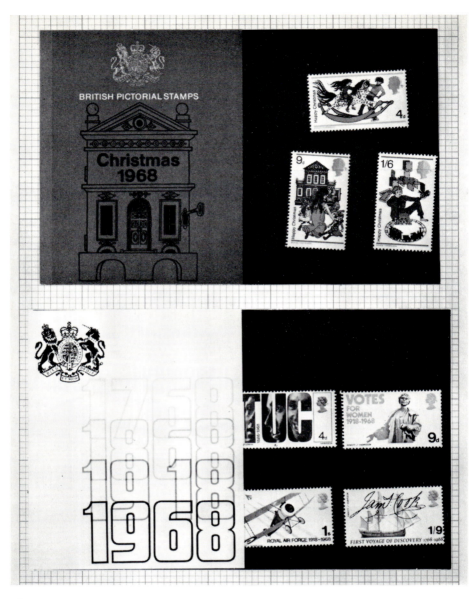

26. PRESENTATION PACKS
Now an accepted part of the new issue scene. *Upper:* Christmas 1968;
Lower: first anniversary series

hibitions, at the special Post Office attached to such events, until exhausted. Four different versions were on sale in window envelopes with short printed details included as an insert. At 10s 6d, the 'Eighteen Low Value Stamps' contained all those on sale in 1960. A mixed lot, all values from $\frac{1}{2}$d to 1s 6d were with crown watermark, except for 1$\frac{1}{2}$d and 11d on the obsolete St Edward crown paper. 'Four High Value Stamps', cost 38 shillings, and 'Sixteen Experimental Stamps', made up of eight graphite and eight phosphor-graphite, contained the sheet versions from $\frac{1}{2}$d to 4$\frac{1}{2}$d. Finally 'Twelve Regional Stamps', at 7s 3d included all such items on sale in 1960. Complete packs are very scarce today.

Then a gap, until the first of the modern packs were issued in conjunction with the Shakespeare set. Intermittently at first, and later for all issues except for some single-value stamps, these presentation packs have become part of the current philatelic scene. There are also a number of combined issue folders, offering for example a complete range of the year's special issues. These packs are heavily promoted, with full-page colour advertisements in the national press, and there are alternatives, with insets in translation, for sale abroad.

Probably the greatest single event of the 1960s, as it affected the collector, was the establishment of the National Postal Museum. R. M. Phillips of Brighton generously donated his superb collection of nineteenth-century British Postage Stamps. Certainly the best in private hands, it was only excelled by the privileged collections of the Queen, and that of the Post Office itself. Mr Phillips also donated substantial funds to help establish the museum as a centre for collectors who wished to study, research or just enjoy his treasures. To this nucleus, the Post Office added its own unique collection of sheets, from the reference archives, and their world file of stamps from the Universal Postal Union.

From humble beginnings in a small room, it has already expanded to offer areas for changing exhibitions, a library and reading room, and a gallery for the basic permanent display. Sited at the London Chief Office, St Martins-le-Grand, London E.C.1, collectors are welcomed during normal opening hours. Late-night visits can be arranged, for societies and other study groups.

British collectors can enjoy the museum's archive accumulation of unique essays, proofs and colour trials, which form the story of the development of the Machin Head design. These have been on show, as part of a special exhibition, and are still available for inspection by philatelic students.

The Stamp Advisory Committee was established in its present form in January 1968 to advise on the selection of suitable designs. Drawing its members from a wide range of professions and interests, it included representatives of the hobby—the first time collectors have had any say in the stamps they buy.

What then of the Post Office today, and its attitude towards the collector? Great strides have been made, but it would be complacent to assume that a perfect situation exists. There are still delays when ordering by post, there are problems when slight changes take place in current stamps. There is room for improvement in the supply of shades and of marginal markings but not all collectors would agree. There is a substantial minority who still wish the Post Office to leave some of the thrill of the chase; they do not want everything to be sold by rote.

Today's collector is offered an unrivalled range of facilities. His predecessors in any other age would marvel at what is done on his behalf. Some post offices abroad do more for the collector than ours. The majority do far less.

11

Guernsey and Jersey

Given the option to do so, Guernsey and Jersey decided to run their own postal services. This was made possible when the control of the British Post Office was transferred from a department of the Crown to an independent state corporation. The islands started operations as unilateral administrations from 1 October 1969.

Guernsey Bailiwick, as the stamps are inscribed, issued no less than 23 stamps on the first day, 16 for postage and seven postage dues. A common theme runs through the lower values up to 2s 6d, placed on sale that day. The Queen looks across at one of her predecessors, these earlier monarchs spanning the ages from Edward the Confessor to Queen Victoria. Inset are views, maps and objects associated with the Bailiwick.

Castle Cornet appears on the $\frac{1}{2}$d, a Martello Tower on the $1\frac{1}{2}$d and 2s 6d, while a map embracing not only the island of Guernsey but also Herm, Jethou, Sark and Alderney appears on both 1d and 1s 6d. The badge of Guernsey was chosen for 5d and 1s, of Alderney on 3d and 6d, and of Sark on the 9d. The Guernsey Lily, already familiar from the regional stamps, is the centrepiece for 4d and 1s 9d.

Views from the sea on the higher values capture the tiny harbour of Sark (5s), the harbour at Alderney (10s), and St Peter Port (£1). These values have the Queen's cameo head superimposed in the lower right-hand corner.

Printing was shared by two firms, Harrison and Sons for stamps up to 2s 6d, and Delerieu of Paris for the three remaining values. The French firm also produced the seven postage dues,

1d, 2d, 3d, 4d, 5d, 6d and 1s, with their common view of Castle Cornet and the figures of denomination superimposed.

Unfortunately, pressure of work at the printers delayed production of these stamps. In addition the Bailiwick had mounted an extended publicity campaign to sell their new stamps. Orders came flocking in from all over the world, yet they could not be prepared in advance. Although they had modelled their services on, and taken advice from, the British Philatelic Bureau, the late delivery of the new stamps meant that it was impossible to make up orders in readiness. Some arrived only hours before the vesting day. Some were only sufficient to meet normal public demand.

On the great day itself, such activity as the island had never seen before burst out at all post offices. Long queues were formed at the Philatelic Bureau and, to make matters worse, the two odd halfpenny values, $\frac{1}{2}$d and 1$\frac{1}{2}$d, were in limited supply, for the Guernsey Post Office had rashly announced that there was to be no second printing of these particular denominations. Meeting no legitimate postal need, these values were an anachronism resulting from plans made one year earlier. Speculators rushed in for them, buying not by the stamp, or even by the sheet, but by the bundle whenever they could. There was a real danger that the advance postal orders would not be met, and rationing was introduced. If this was not enough, further confusion was caused when widespread publicity was given to the error in design of the two map stamps. The 1d and 1s 6d had the latitude wrongly incribed as 40° 30′, instead of 49° 30′. This positioned Guernsey in the middle of Spain, near Madrid. These too were in demand as the purchasers rightly surmised that this would have to be corrected.

Meanwhile thousands of postal orders, some sent in months before, still awaited attention. Hard-worked staff were harassed as telephone and postal enquiries bombarded them, and it was weeks before all the mint stamps were despatched. Even the first-day covers were still being serviced over a month later, making a mockery of the name and postmark. Slowly the dust subsided. Booklets had been promised, but failed to arrive. Eventually they were placed on sale from 12 December 1969. Attractively designed covers featured old Guernsey troop uniforms. Three separate editions, 2s, 4s and 6s, contained

27. A CARD FROM SANTA CLAUS
Every Christmas, letters addressed to Santa Claus at imaginary
addresses are answered. The illustration shows the card used in 1969

28. JERSEY

On 1 October, 1969, Jersey issued its own stamps, on taking over its own postal affairs. Typical definitives, an example of the postal due series, with the first commemorative highlighting the swing away from the British series sheetlets of one stamp, with a surrounding border. Three 4d, two 5d and two 1d stamps made up the 2s version, and the higher valued booklets contained similar proportions. As forecast the 1d now showed the correct latitude, although it was not until some weeks later that the revised 1d and 1s 6d appeared in sheets. Later booklets had new cover pictures in line with the policy to change them periodically.

Only one item of stationery was issued at the beginning. Adapting the design of the £1 value, a 9d airletter with impressed stamp was on sale. An unusual sideline may be made from the official envelopes used by the Bailiwick and by the Guernsey Philatelic Bureau with its distinctive map franks.

A second printing of 5s, 10s and £1 was made with finer perforations, 14 instead of 12 holes every two centimetres. Decimal equivalents of 25p and 50p had already been planned when the second shilling printing was ordered.

A moderate commemorative policy had been agreed. Four stamps for Major General Sir Isaac Brock started the ball rolling. He was at one time Governor and Commander in Chief of Upper Canada, to be killed in the defence of Queenstown, by American forces under General Van Rennselaer. The stamps were issued on 1 December 1969. Special series for 1970 included the 25th anniversary of the liberation of the Channel Islands, pictorials spotlighting agriculture and horticulture, and a feature issue covering churches from the four islands of the Bailiwick. Special postmarks include the 117th anniversary of the oldest pillar box in the British Isles, at Union Street, Guernsey on 9 February 1970.

Jersey's story contains similar strands of woe, with all its good intentions thwarted by the non-arrival of stamps in advance. The island planned for 15 postage, four commemorative, six postage due, three stamp booklets and four items of stationery, all on 1 October 1969. A worldwide publicity campaign surprised and gratified them. Lacking expertise, Jersey also called on the British Bureau, and a simple yet comprehensive order form was devised. Ready to go into action, yet stymied by the late delivery, orders mounted. A total of 32 varieties and apparently endless permutations made it a back-breaking job to clear the backlog.

Jersey shared their printing contract for the definitives

between Harrison and Sons Ltd and Courvoisier of Switzerland. Unlike Guernsey, all their horizontal stamps share a common frame, and a comparison of similar stamps from the two printers showed that they were equal masters of their craft.

Mostly local views, Elizabeth Castle on the ½d, Portlet Bay peering from the 2d and La Corbiere Lighthouse on the 3d, are reminders that on an island one is never far from the sea. Mont Orgueil Castle is seen at night, with lights reflecting on the water on the 4d, while the 1s continues the theme with another view by day. These last three subjects had been used before in the locally produced wartime pictorials, but the monochrome of 25 years earlier failed to do them justice.

An inland hill, La Hougue Bie, largest and most spectacular of the neolithic remains, appears on the 1d, arms and royal mace share the 5d and a Jersey cow placidly looking out from the 6d vary the selection. For the two denominations most likely to be used on foreign mail, 9d and 1s 6d, there is a map showing the relation of the island both to France and England, with Jersey boldly marked in red. A head and shoulders view, in upright format, was chosen for the 1s 9d.

Jersey Airport on the 2s 6d, the 5s Legislative Chamber and the 10s Royal Court completes the pictorial section. An extended portrait of the Queen appears on the top value, £1, and the head is adapted for use on all values. It was specially commissioned by the island from Cecil Beaton. All four values in common design made up the first commemorative series for the inauguration of the Jersey Post Office. It was one of those clever ideas, an envelope and stamp with first-day postmark. Look carefully, and on the stamp is seen another envelope with another stamp and so on, until the detail gets too small and is lost.

A third firm, Bradbury, Wilkinson, was responsible for printing the postage due labels. Small-size, the three lowest values have a simple numeral design, incribed 'Postage Due', and the 1s, 2s 6d and 5s are labelled 'To Pay'. Inset is a simplified road map of the island. These values do not seem to have been chosen with care. As an example, an unpaid letter attracting 8d due would need at least three labels.

Aerogrammes are printed with the normal 9d stamp, in blue. Three sizes of registered envelope carry an embossed Tudor

Rose design, with additional information. Booklets at 2s, 7s and 10s were placed on sale, with pictorial covers. Because the 2s booklet had to fit the coin-operated machines inherited from the British Post Office, the format is similar to those of Guernsey. Five at 4d, and four at 1d make up the contents, one stamp to a page, with surrounding border. The other two booklets are more conventional, with varying quantities of 4d, 5d and 1d denominations, identical in all respects to sheet issues.

A regular, but not too frequent commemorative programme has been settled, and decimal values have replaced the old shilling and pence denominations.

These two small islands entered the philatelic field with untold goodwill. Not only collectors of Great Britain, ready and willing to extend their collections, but also philatelists throughout the world, saw the opportunity to start at the beginning. It was unfortunate that the possibility of late delivery of stamps was overlooked.

It is clear that both Guernsey and Jersey have learnt from their mistakes. We are unlikely to see any more stamps like the $\frac{1}{2}$d and $1\frac{1}{2}$d with no clear postal function to fulfill, and no coin to buy them. New sets are always in the pipeline, comparing favourably in frequency and value with other countries. As visitors stream in, to sample the summer sunshine, they will use these stamps on letters home; some no doubt will be converted to collecting. Then the earlier issues will be wanted. While they are still relatively common, that is the right time to make sure of the handful so far issued, especially the obsolete sterling series. Guernsey and Jersey are part of Europe, and part of the Commonwealth, two areas with strong loyalties. And for the keen collector there is always the possibility of a few days over there, to get up to date at the post office counter in person!

12

Cinderellas

With few strictly limited exceptions, carriage of mail is a Post Office monopoly. Nevertheless there are numerous examples of semi-official or purely private stamps, which may form the nucleus of a Cinderella collection, so-called because they are too often neglected, despised, remaining unknown because the main catalogues ignore their existence.

Chief among these are the special airway letters stamps issued by British European Airways for use on packages carried on their internal domestic flights. An airway letter is a particular form of express carriage, permitting fast transmission of correspondence and small articles from one end of the country to another, if there is an airport or town terminal close by. Such packets can be handed in either at the central terminus or at the airfield, there to be conveyed by the next scheduled flight, and if need be carried into the centre of the town at its destination. It can be retained to be called for, or posted in the nearest letter box, but in either case it must bear full Post Office postage, in addition to the airway letter stamps. This is compulsory, even though it may never pass through the normal mails.

British European Airways issued their first stamps in a pleasant design showing a map of the United Kingdom, with a superimposed BEA symbol. A simple inscription, the denomination, and a space with the prefix 'To', completed the wording. These stamps were printed by Harrison and Sons, the same printers as the ordinary low-value issues, and were issued in January 1951, in 6d, 11d and 1s 4d denominations. These three rates depended only upon weight, covering bands up to two

29. GUERNSEY—I

Eight of the first definitive stamps. The ½d and 1½d were sold out
almost immediately, and the 1d had to be replaced when it was
noticed that the wrong latitude was inscribed

30. GUERNSEY—2

Higher values from the definitive series, the first commemorative set, and one of the postage due series

ounces, four ounces and one pound.

Soon after issue, new rates were introduced, but rather than print new values the airline decided to surcharge current stocks. For one week this was done at local offices by varying emergency methods, and then on 14 May 1951 the stamps were reissued after treatment at a central point, the surcharge consisting simply of a rubber stamp, reading 'Plus 1d' on the two lower values and 'Plus 2d' on the highest. They were still in use on the accession of Queen Elizabeth and remained so until 25 November 1953.

Further carriage increases brought forth new stamps, new values and a new design. Large, 54 by 35mm featuring the three crowns' arms flanked by a decorative scroll, they retained the earlier sets colours. 8d green, 1s 2d blue and 1s 9d red were replaced at a fast and furious pace over the next few years. Higher postal fees and new stamps seemed to arrive every few months. In fact they were: 1 September 1954, broadly the same design, 9d, 1s 3d and 1s 11d; 27 June 1956, a smaller-format revised stamp, 10d, 1s 5d and 2s 2d; 1 July 1957, 11d, 1s 6d and 2s 4d.

A few years of comparative stability came to a close with BEA's first and only commemorative, a single 11d, valid for use on one day only, 9 September 1961. This was the day that they re-enacted the historic first official airmail flight between Hendon and Windsor, 50 years before. Cards similar to those used on this flight celebrating the Coronation of King George V were prepared and a helicopter flew over the route. Even the ordinary Post Office stamps were treated on arrival to a special slogan postmark.

4 October 1961 saw a plain utilitarian label, issued for the new tariff, valued at 1s, 1s 8d and 2s 7d. A later series, still in use in 1970, had these values unchanged when the plain pattern was cast aside in favour of a symbolical aircraft, on 27 May 1964. The era of cheap express airmail came to an end on 1 July 1967, when fees shot up to 3s 7d, 4s 3d and 5s 2d. These arbitrary rates were no doubt chosen by the three values of stamps on sale. Each of these charges could be made up by adding a 2s 7d stamp to each denomination.

With decimalisation only ten months away, new stamps were placed on sale from 1 May 1970. Showing the flash that appears on their fleet aircraft, the three denominations of 3s 7d, 4s 3d and 5s 2d were designed by F. H. K. Henrion. The airline serviced a number of first-day covers to a variety of destinations, including the Channel Islands. In addition a presentation pack was made available for the first time.

Who uses such stamps, and this esoteric service? If truth be told, hardly anyone. The airline admitted that the only source of publicity is the *Post Office Guide*, and precious few would-be users will bother to scan the pages, ready for that odd day in a thousand when some urgent document must be in Glasgow, a few hours after it leaves London. In the 1962 post office strike there were a number of reports of firms using this scheme, but on normal days only a handful at most will fly. For such mail, 4s, made up of 3s 7d airway letter fee and 5d first-class postage, seems cheap enough. Cambrian Airways, when they took over the operation of some internal routes previously operated only by BEA, inherited the airway service. For some time they used their predecessor's stamps, and then issued their own. Plain, undistinctive, in the same format and denominations as the BEA 1961 set, they were available from 2 December 1964.

A similar facility is to be found within the pages of the *Post Office Guide*—the railway letter service. This scheme has undergone modifications recently, but in essence permits a letter of up to one pound weight to be handed in at any station to be carried by train to any other station, there to be held for collection, or to be posted on arrival. The journey must be continuous, without change of station. British Rail do not consider it worthwhile to issue special stamps for this particular operation, and use parcel labels with manuscript or machine entries. It was not always so. Back in the days of the independent lines, many a small company issued its own 2d, 3d or 4d stamp, although conforming in general to the standard approved design.

After the war there was a movement to preserve small lines, often narrow-gauge, and to operate them under steam. One such, in the foothills of Cader Idris, is the Talyllyn Railway, the line that nationalisation forgot. When it was about to close, or rather collapse after years of neglect, with no funds available to replenish line or stock, an enthusiastic preservation organisation took over, refurbishing route, coaches and stations. It made a considerable profit, but most of the supporting services are run on a voluntary basis by their membership.

Incorporated by Act of Parliament, and overlooked by the nationalisation bill of 1947, it remains a statutory railway company. They invoked the standing agreement between such lines and the Post Office, and started up their own railway letter service on 23 May 1957. This permitted the posting of letters at any of the manned stations on the six-mile line, for transmission to the sea terminus at Towyn, Merioneth. Most such letters are souvenirs, and are posted there, but there is an obligation on the part of British Rail to carry them far and wide over their own network.

Six pictorial 11d designs were released in May 1957, each appearing once in a sheet of six. Each stamp exists in either green or red—a total of 12 distinct stamps for this first service. Unhappily the rate was raised almost immediately to 1s. With 12 stamps, but only one value, they were in a quandary, solved temporarily with an extra-charge rubber stamp, and later by surcharging the sheets with a 1s overprint. The original 11d stamps are now very scarce and are rarely available. Only 448 of each distinct stamp can exist.

1,052 of each surcharged stamp were issued, and this is a mere fleabite, considering that they were on sale for some seven years. They are not hard to find, for fair stocks were left on withdrawal and sold to collectors as souvenirs. In 1965 a 1s denomination was produced in honour of 100 years in the life of the company, and it was retained for regular service until the rate went up to 1s 1d in 1966. Two surcharges were made, first in red which proved unsatisfactory, and then in green. A competition in the philatelic press yielded a new design, and the winner was commissioned to produce a companion stamp. Featuring two different old engines, they were printed se-tenant on the sheet. Constant increases in rates, often at little notice, were annoying, and to avoid future embarrassment make-up 1d and 6d denominations were added, primarily for heavier packages but also for possible rises in cost.

They did not appear soon enough, for British Rail decided upon a new fee, a few weeks before a 1s 2d Prince of Wales commemorative and a multicolour 1s 6d were issued. This was the final straw, and the Talyllyn Railway rebelled, deciding not to charge the higher prices until after they had serviced their advance orders for the new stamps and covers. Then, and only then, did they bring their rates in line with Big Brother.

There was no hurry to bring out new denominations, now that penny stamps were on sale. In 1970 1s 3d and 1s 7d stamps were added to the range.

In 1969 two other railway lines decided to avail themselves of the privilege of accepting and carrying railway letters. They realised that this could be a valuable source of extra income, a pertinent point for societies such as these, always dependent on voluntary offerings. Their only real expenses were the printing costs of the stamps.

First on the scene, from 28 May 1969, was the Festiniog Railway, an old slate line now carrying passengers with professional expertise. Observation and refreshment coaches included, the trains wend their way up the mountain side from Portmadoc, Caernarvonshire to the mist-shrouded slate town of Blaenau Festiniog, although the last few miles are still to be completed. Some of the original track has been drowned through an electricity pumped storage scheme. The Company planned not only a 1s 2d stamp, but also a suite of three lower values, to meet the heavier weight bands, and to forestall any later inflationary rises.

It was just as well that they foresaw the possibility, for only two days before the service was due to swing into operation, the rate did go up, without warning. Suddenly the philatelic cover department was faced with the need to add an extra 1d to every cover. The first set, showing railway scenes over the years, has been reprinted many times, with differences of importance to specialists. One commemorative, 1s 3d, was released in 1969 to commemorate the centenary of Robert Francis Fairlie, responsible for the invention of a remarkable twin engine, which faces both ways at once. One solution to the problem of turning at the end of the line. A definitive 1s 3d was added in 1970.

Ravenglass and Eskdale, with seven miles of line in Cumberland, followed suit on 1 July 1969 with a single stamp, and the remarkable large-size black 1s 2d, with design outlined in white, also showed an engine. Originally it had been intended to have the stamp printed in the normal way, but detail was too fine for satisfactory reproduction. Quite by chance they

31. BRITISH EUROPEAN AIRWAYS
The first series, 6d and 11d. The third series 8d. Special one day
11d to mark the 50th anniversary of the Hendon–Windsor airmail
flight. The first pictorial 1s with a Trident aircraft

32. TALYLLYN RAILWAY

First row: Provisionals to meet the 1s 1d railway fee.

Second row: Two 1s 2d definitives.

Third row: Prince of Wales 1s 2d commemorative, and pictorial 1s 6d.

Fourth row: Additional 1d and 6d values to meet changes in letter
rates

found that in reverse a viable possibility emerged. They too had been caught out by the increase to 1s 3d, between planning and issue. Their solution was to add an explanatory handstamp to covers, denoting an additional one penny paid. A straight-forward 1s 3d, in more conventional format was placed on sale in 1970.

Scattered around the coastline of the British Isles lie small islands, supporting perhaps a dozen or so permanent residents. Some never see a postman. They are too far away to receive a service that most of us take for granted. Instead the inhabitants must make their own arrangements to collect and despatch their letters.

Some of these remote places have issued stamps to prepay charges introduced for the carriage of mail, helping to defray the cost of transport to the mainland. To avoid misrepresentation the trade organisations require their dealer members to describe such stamps as 'local carriage labels'. Unlike airway and railway letter stamps, these local issues must be placed on the reverse of the envelope. In addition normal stamps prepay ordinary postal charges. Organisers of these services find that they must take special care, so that the day visitors, arriving at the more popular islands in their thousands, do not fall foul of the regulations. Otherwise, letters with locals on the front may be returned by the Post Office as unacceptable.

One such island is Lundy, nestling in the Bristol Channel, 24 miles from the nearest mainland port. In 1929 the owner decided to issue a short set of stamps, featuring the commonest bird in residence—puffins. Serious collectors tended to treat them with uninterested amusement, except for a brave few who studied, catalogued and wrote about them. Interest was sustained by the odd commemorative or airmail issue, and printings rarely exceeded a few thousands. Just enough to satisfy mail and collecting requirements.

A last-minute decision to issue a set for the Coronation celebrations in 1953 only proved practicable by overprinting basic stamps. Unexpected and unwarranted was the total quantity prepared—120,000 sets. Seven different values, $\frac{1}{2}$ to 12 puffins (the local name for pennies), savoured of exploitation. Later sets in the 1950s were announced with even larger printings—half a million or more of some. Puffins converted into pennies means big profits, and from the considerable remainder stocks that have been placed on the market, it seems that some entrepreneur secured the contract. In exchange for the payment of the printing bills, a small supply was provided for the island post office, and the rest placed on the market. In comparison with these speculative sets, the original one puffin, issued in 1929 and also printed to the tune of half a million, lasted well into 1969, a span of 40 years.

Lundy fell from favour, and although sets since 1964 have been produced in smaller quantities, interest has failed to revive. Taken over by the National Trust in 1969, the future of stamps on Lundy may be in the melting pot.

Three miles from Guernsey lies the Channel Island of Herm. They too began to issue stamps, to cover the conveyance of mail to St Peter Port, from 1949. Their celebration of the Coronation was far more modest—four overprints and only 2,000 sets were prepared, to be followed by a second printing of a similar number to satisfy the demand. But later the blight that had affected Lundy struck Herm too. Half a million triangular stamp sets, 12 different designs of flora and fauna, were suddenly foisted on the unsuspecting public in October 1954. It was as well that the holiday season was over, as these shapes are so difficult to separate. So few were actually delivered for postal use, that Herm had run out of stocks of the four doubles, equivalent to one halfpenny, in June 1955, before the onset of the summer rush.

They seemed to have learnt their lesson, for later issues covering a variety of celebrations were confined to a few thousand overprinted sets each time. Suddenly the Europa boom was at its height, and around a quarter of a million sets were printed. This was the beginning of the rot, from which this attractive little island, with its unusual inexpensive issues, never really recovered. Its last stamps appeared just before vesting day, October 1969, when Guernsey took over the postal services in the area. Banning all local issues, from whatever quarter, within the Bailiwick, it did at least provide an official post office on Herm.

Other islets have also organised their own colourful issues, and each year seems to bring fresh ones to the fold. Jethou, just across the sound from Herm, joined the handwagon in 1960.

At first discrete, they were tempted by the money to be made from frequent commemorative sets. Their last issue came on the last day of their service, for they too were forced to close down on 30 September 1969, leaving the island without the benefit of a post office for the handful of permanent residents.

Pabay and Stroma, islands in Scotland, seem to share a common need for local stamps, and they share the same designs too. But when the identical expensive set, except for colour and island name, appear with and without perforations, and also in miniature sheet form, it becomes self-evident that any real postal need has become subordinated to the desire to accommodate collectors.

Typical of these stamp-producing areas is the Calf of Man, with its private postal arrangements to the Isle of Man. This has operated for a number of years, and in 1966 the Director of the Manx Museum and the National Trust explained that it is not run or financed by them directly, but operates under an agreement with the Trust. It seems likely that the prime motif is to sell as many copies as possible for the smallest outlay. What other interpretation can be placed on the reappearance time and time again, in all sorts of formats, of a standarised design bearing Winston Churchill's head. They come with various overprints, in differing hues, expressed in the non-existent if quaint 'murreys' currency.

Few of these local stamps are now produced primarily for postal use. Collectors' purchases, more often than not, outnumber any genuine local sale, if in fact at some of the remoter places there are any sold at all.

No monopoly is held by the Post Office for the carriage of parcels, and a number of common carriers offer this facility. British Rail no longer bothers with stamps, but many provincial bus companies run extensive and highly organised services with agents in every town within their area. Their plain, functional labels have had little published about them, and only now are the facts being uncovered by a brave, tiny minority of cinderella collectors.

More common are the labels used by the Commodore Shipping Service between Guernsey and Alderney or Sark. Initially using plain typeset labels, they went pictorial in 1961, and also managed to celebrate the ubiquitous Europa theme.

For a shipping service, their choice of aircraft in the designs of later series seemed strangely out of place, and to save money on needless printing plates, such stamps suffered countless overprints and surcharges.

Labels issued by the Peoples League for the Defence of Freedom lie in a different category. This was a ginger group centred around the readership of the *New Daily*, who attempted to organise a comprehensive system during the postal strike of 1962. In the first few hours some letters were carried, but the Postmaster-General indicated that, despite the interruption in service, the monopoly remained. They switched their attention to a nationwide parcel delivery, and according to contemporary accounts it functioned efficiently. Stamps were issued, and with subtypes they form a compact group. The basic series, on sale at all their depots, was offered to readers of the *New Daily* at the conclusion of operations, at face value. Some remainders seem to have leaked onto the market, and are relatively common. More than 30,000 parcels were delivered during the two-week emergency.

All the stamps described in this chapter are of local interest and are not fully fledged postage stamps, in the official sense. Their importance varies considerably, from the BEA stamps with a pedigree to be expected from a nationalised industry, down to some coloured pieces of paper prepared for Carn Iar, an islet off the north west of Scotland, 16 miles from Ullapool, offered for sale in 1965 for £4,750. No buildings were included, for they did not exist!

Many philatelists will include the railway stamps without hesitation, and some of the more reputable local carriage labels are favoured with space in the album. Unfortunately too many of the other issues are sold to unsuspecting youngsters, hypnotised by the bright colours and bargain prices. Their worth in both financial and philatelic terms is that of printed coloured gummed paper.

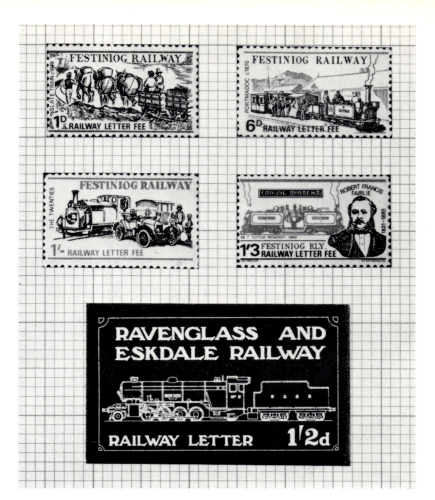

33. MODERN RAILWAY LETTER STAMPS
Festiniog Railway definitives, and their first commemorative
marking 100 years in service of Fairlies Patent Locomotive.
Ravenglass and Eskdale's unusual first stamp

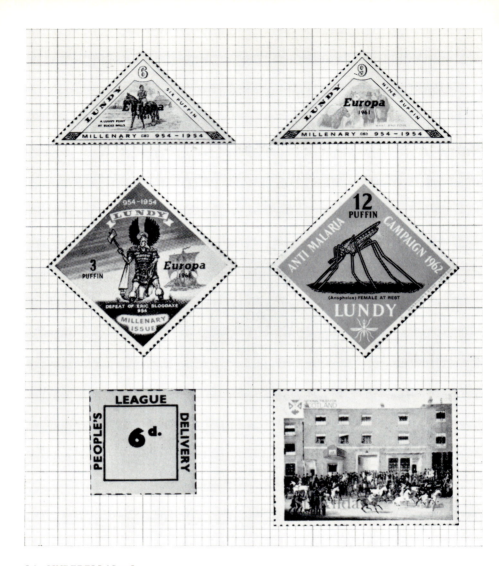

34. CINDERELLAS—I
Unusual shaped multicolour commemoratives from Lundy Island
in the Bristol Channel. A functional 6d label used by the People's
League for the Defence of Freedom parcel service. A modern label,
with one eye on the collector, produced for St Kilda

13

Postmarks and Postal Markings

Large commercial firms cannot be bothered with stamps on their mail. Meter markings are invariably used. At one time it was even suggested that the growth of impressed markings foreshadowed the demise of postage stamps. These prophets of doom have yet to see their predictions come true.

A select few companies are permitted by the Post Office to sell or hire meter machines to customers and details will be found in the current edition of the *Post Office Guide*. This annual publication, containing so much information of interest to collectors generally, lays down the conditions under which correspondence is accepted. Mail is normally handed in at a specified office, or mailed direct to the sorting centre in special envelopes. Postage must be paid in advance, and machines are preset with the amount in credit. Returns are required weekly, and as a further safeguard all machines must be inspected at least twice every six months.

Franking impressions include the date and name of the town of posting, an optional advertising or informative message, and the amount paid in postage. For two years prior to decimal conversion day, all new machines, and some older ones, showed the amount in pence only. Heavy parcels requiring 12s 6d franking would be printed 150, without any indication of the unit of currency. Pence was implied, and after D Day it was similarly inferred that the value was in new pence.

Large postings can be made at selected offices without bothering with meters or postage stamps. Instead, the total due may be handed over in money. Letters and packets are franked with a handstamp or machine impression. It used to be the custom to indicate the amount paid, but now it is more usual simply to indicate the class of service required.

Official mail, especially in the larger towns, is similarly treated but with an 'Official Paid' indication. According to Universal Postal Union regulations, all such frankings, private or postal, must be in red ink.

Very large postings in bulk attract substantial discounts. They are routed by second-class mail, and certain conditions are imposed, but with these discounts rising to 25 per cent, for a quarter of a million or more packets, they are well worth while. At one time these packets received the normal Post Office frank, but latterly it has become customary to incorporate a small printed rectangular permit, usually but not always in black. Letters from the National Giro, for instance, are printed with the inscription 'Postage Paid Liverpool Serial 12', within a framed border.

From these markings, which are of interest to only a small band of collectors, it is a short step to postmarks. These are studied in depth by more than one society, and a general record of all sorts of postal impressions is maintained by the British Postmark Society.

With slogans and advertising messages commonplace, it is difficult to recall that in 1953 nearly every slogan was sponsored by the Post Office or another government department. In the first eight years about 150 slogans were noted. Over 50 pages were needed to supplement this list in *Slogan Postmarks of the United Kingdom,* for those issued in 1968 alone.

It was the practice for many years to carry the slogan, or message section of a machine postmark, to the right of the circular town die. When local authorities and other interested regional organisations were allowed to sponsor their own publicity, there was the obvious disadvantage that the message would be in part lost, where it overlapped the stamp. This was remedied by transposing the slogan to the left.

A specialised listing of slogan marks divides them into seven sections. It distinguishes between general slogans, which vary from nationwide campaigns to the one-time, one-town advertisement for a particular event, and the local publicity message, paid for by a tourist office or district council. Included in separate sections are such specialised fields as exceptional usage, when a slogan was impressed out of normal time, and the errors where part of the cancellation was inserted upside down. Remaining sections cover those used by the National Savings Bank, Maritime marks, and the miscellaneous ones that refuse to fit into any regular section. Typical of this last small group are the first day of issue marks, and also the franks in red reading 'Reindeerland', used on Christmas cards from Santa Claus replying to the young children who write into him.

Slogan postmarks offer a vast field. Interesting sidelines can be built up from specialising in certain types. Themes can vary from Post Office advertisements to modes of transport. Examples of Post Office exhortations connected with postal services and postage stamps include 'Postage on letters to Europe 4d'; 'Save time, buy 2½d stamps in books 3/9 a book'; 'Buy stamps in books'; and '6d Recorded Delivery cheap effective'.

Transport could include '50th anniversary of the first aerial post 1911-1961'; '1863-1963 Underground a century of London's service'; 'Harlow Motorists Week May 12-19'; and 'Gosport Hovershow 66'.

Even if no attempt is made to collect more than one example of each slogan it will take many months to build up even a representative showing, and much, much longer before some semblance of completeness comes into view. It is cheap enough to collect current specimens. All that is needed is a good source of supply, such as a large office. They will usually be associated with current definitive stamps, and even the most collecting-conscious competitor will not bother to give them a second look.

Some themes are hard to find. The Welsh National Eisteddfod has on occasions been publicised at a limited number of offices. Bridgend 1948 was advertised on 12 machines only, and Rhyl 1953 just on one. This Rhyl item is rare even though it had a life of 28 days. All the early Eisteddfod postmarks are in short supply and in great demand.

Complementary to slogan marks are special handstamps, now freely available to non-commercial organisations. Often they will be used on mail posted in one postbox only, or one afternoon. Rubber dies with fixed dates, or for longer periods steel dies, may be ordered. These cancelling devices remain the property of the Post Office, and never leave their hands. Stamp clubs holding conventions and exhibitions often sponsor them, producing cacheted envelopes and selling them at a profit to supplement funds. Their use has grown. About one dozen appeared in 1954. Today this number may be exceeded during the course of one busy summer weekend.

Handstamps for stamp exhibitions, national or local, are popular. The Philatelic Congress of Great Britain has led the way for many a year, and the latest fashion seems to dictate a new design daily.

Handstamps are in daily use. At the National Postal Museum all letters deposited in the posting box within the display area are carefully treated by hand, a boon to new issue collectors when no special arrangements have been made. The first day of issue circular handstamp replaced the first machine marks. At first rather large, it was reduced to a more compact size, beginning with the long Battle of Hastings set.

Collectors chase many of the almost unknown handstamps of limited use. Every night except Saturday, a network of special trains threads through the countryside. Carrying a special coach or coaches, one will have a familiar red letter box peering out from the side. Mail posted there, with a small supplementary fee, gets immediate attention and is almost certain to be delivered to any town en route, the following morning. These Travelling Post Offices each have their own handstamps, with such explicit descriptions as 'London-York-Edinburgh TPO'; 'Manchester-Glasgow SC' (for Sorting Carriage); or 'Up Special'. Incidentally all these postmarks include the date of departure, and some clever collectors with new issues of stamps purchased at the all-night post office in London, would rush to stations within 50 miles or so of London to post their covers on inbound services. This forced the authorities to use extra handstamps on such days, with the actual date, and the distinguishing letters 'AM'.

Ships can be as rich a source as trains. All mail from abroad is allowed to be prepaid with stamps of the country of registry of the vessel. Such mail, and a fair amount of British postage stamped letters, receive a postmark reading 'Paquebot'. This, the French spelling of packet boat, is a reminder of the days

35. CINDERELLAS—2
Labels in use in the Channel Islands. They covered the carriage
element to nearest British Post Office from Herm or Jethou, and the
parcel postage on the inter-island shipping services

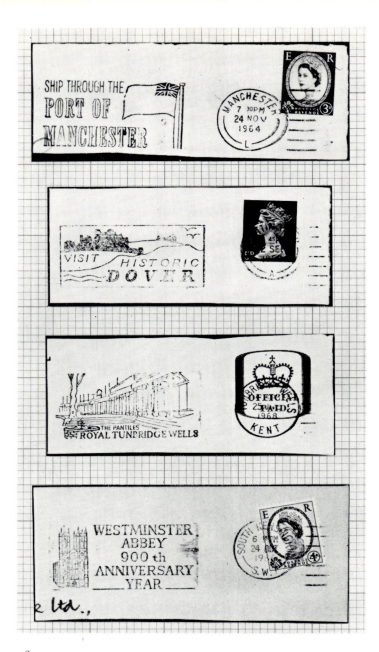

36. SLOGAN POSTMARKS
Pictorial postmarks may be sponsored by local authorities.
The Dover slogan was actually used in Nottingham, paid
for by Dover

when all international letters from and to Great Britain relied upon such letter packets, or boats. Apart from Southampton, where the trans-Atlantic liners can disgorge many bags of mail at every visit, these marks are not easy to secure. On cross-Channel ferries it is often simpler for the purser of a ship to carry the mail back on the next voyage; and post it in the usual way.

This simplified account can only scratch the surface of a story which is as intriguing and rewarding as the collecting of stamps themselves. Cancellations with a difference certainly embellish a collection.

14

Printing, Errors and Varieties

Stamp collecting is one of those strange hobbies where the faulty commands high prices. In other fields, the second-rate are rejected, fetching a fraction of the perfect price. Not so with stamps. An error of missing colour or perforation can raise the price ten thousand fold. Major finds sell for hundreds of pounds, while the normal version may be worth just a few pence. Values are determined by the number available, and these high realisations are a tribute to the accuracy and to the careful inspection techniques at the printers.

Most British stamps are printed by the photogravure process. The finished drawing is photographed, and after the negative has been retouched it is repeatedly photographed by an automatic 'step and repeat' camera. This produces a large sheet, the multi-positive, containing perhaps 600 stamp-size images. These are carefully checked, and from somewhere in the array a master single or double sheet is masked off, ready for the next stage.

A sheet of paper, called the carbon tissue, is then spread with bichromated gelantine, a chemical which becomes insoluble on exposure to light. This tissue is first exposed behind a fine grid of horizontal and vertical lines, and then again to the multipositive. The first step leaves a fine screen of dots unexposed, and the second step causes them to receive varying strengths of light. Now the tissue is placed in contact with the printing cylinder and the gelantine is washed off. Some remains, and after cleaning up the cylinder and painting out those parts not required, the copper is etched with perchloride of iron.

Acid eats away the unprotected parts, and it is these recesses which will capture the ink as the cylinder revolves. But first, any imperfections must be corrected by hand, the copper is chromium plated to harden the cylinder, and only then is it ready for the printing process. From the recesses the ink is pressed into contact with the paper, and the printed sheet of stamps appears.

A similar principle is used for line-engraved or recess-printed stamps. These two names are used by philatelists more or less indiscriminately. Steel is covered with an acid resisting substance, which is then scored or scratched. The steel is placed in contact with the acid, which eats away the unprotected portions of the surface. The longer the acid contact time, the deeper the etched lines and dots, and the pattern is repeated over and over again until the engraver achieves the desired result.

Once completed, the die is hardened and entered into a soft steel roller, which is in its turn hardened. This roller, with the portions of the design to be printed standing out from the surface, then transfers the impression onto a final soft steel plate. As many impressions as are required are made, before this plate is also hardened, with the portions that will print now recessed. As in the photogravure method, ink settles into the cavities and is forced out under pressure. Under strong magnification the ink can be seen to stand out, away from the flat surface of the paper.

Typography, or letterpress printing, is the exact opposite. The engraver cuts away the portions he does not wish to be printed, and leaves standing the lines of the final design. This die is then struck into a piece of lead, and repeated until the total number of impressions in the sheet have been made and assembled. By electrochemical means, a copper shell is grown, removed, filled with metal to harden it, making a master plate with, say, 240 exact copies of the original die. This master can be copied by further electrochemical processes, to make the final printing plates. Raised surfaces attract ink and are printed onto the paper. Under the pressure the paper is indented where printed, and this too can be observed under magnification.

A fourth process, embossing, was popular in the last century and then fell into relative disuse. For years used only on envelopes, it has recently returned, to provide a portrait on certain commemorative issues. Utilising two dies, one recess, one relief, which fit together, they raise and indent the paper to effect a corrugated impression. Colour comes from inked rollers, passing and repassing over the surface of the die.

Lithography takes full advantage of the property that lines made with greasy ink adhere to stone strongly, removeable only by mechanical force. Non-greasy portions of the surface on the other hand absorb and retain water, and water and grease do not mix. A design is transferred to a dry stone with greasy ink, and the stone is then wetted. The whole surface is covered with greasy ink, but only the design portion retains it, the non-greasy wet sections repelling it. Lithography fell out of favour until quite recently. Modern developments and innovations have brought it back into the fold. The stone has been replaced, in photo-lithography, by a zinc or aluminium plate, and photographic transfer methods have been adopted. To ensure that the whole surface receives the design, offset lithography finds favour. The impression from the plate is transferred to an intermediate rubber blanket, and the resilience enables the offset design to be pressed directly into the texture of the paper. Although a guarded trade secret, the simple basic steps in 'Delacryl', developed by De La Rue, parallel these processes.

Modern British photogravure stamps are either printed on the reel or are sheet-fed. Reel-fed printing takes the paper into the press on a continuous reel, and the printed sheets are later divided. In sheet-fed, the paper is cut to size, and then fed in, one by one.

Reel-fed printing is quicker, but the preparation time to make ready the machines is considerable. The cost of allowing a machine to stand idle during preparation is offset only by the faster printing time for very long runs. Definitives and low-value special issues meet these requirements. In general, high-value commemoratives do not.

Errors can occur. In reel-fed printings the most frequent type is one or more colours missing. The pressure is relaxed to realign the colour register, and although only momentarily, three or four rows are affected. It is unlikely that more than one colour will be missing, but it can happen. Accidental inverted watermarks are theoretically impossible. There are cases where complete reels were fed into the machinery in the reverse direction on purpose. National Productivity Year commemoratives, for example, were printed on paper which showed signs of cracking and there was a real danger of it breaking up completely. To minimise this possibility reels were not rewound. Many examples of the Flower 9d were also found with inverted watermarks, so that at least one, and possibly more reels were inserted in the same way.

Excessive colour displacements are impossible. Although the machine may creep slightly out of true, these are only of the order of a millimetre or so.

Sheet-fed printings are more vulnerable. Missing colours are always being discovered, probably because two sheets are sent through at the same time, and the lower sheet escapes that stage. Inverted watermarks are another phenomena. Stacked for printing, sheets may be easily fed in in reverse. Immediately after printing the ink is still wet, and sometimes very clear offsets of design on the gummed side of the next sheet can occur.

One of the latest types of error to be found is 'phosphor lines omitted'. All low values are automatically treated with phosphor and the automatic equipment can only operate at full efficiency if the stamps are properly printed. Nevertheless there are many examples known with missing phosphor, and they are not readily recognised at the visual inspection stage.

Despite the very full checking procedures, and built-in machine safeguards, major errors will happen. Missing colours are one of the favourites among collectors and the lay public alike. Yet they may vary in importance from the national news story to the relatively insignificant.

Colours partly omitted are not listed by Stanley Gibbons catalogues, which try to draw the line somewhere; but other British specialised listings give them due mention. The first bicolour special issue, Europa 1960, presents a typical example. Part of the green colour is missing from a block of four stamps.

When all the colour is missing, a stamp achieves major error status. Typical, and one of the first, was the spectacular piece on view at the National Stamp Exhibition in London, 1963. Part of the sheet, 76 copies in all, of the National Productivity Year 3d were completely missing the blue. This was the colour used to print the portrait and the variety became known as the Headless Queen. On sale at the exhibition for £85 each, present-day values approach £350. A similar mistake on the 1s 3d was found, but on only a few copies. Values can go down as well as up. Commonwealth Parliamentary Conference 6d stamps of 1961 are known without the gold colour. When first offered they fetched £500 each, but more examples were found and the price dropped to the £100-£150 level.

The stories surrounding such discoveries are often told in the daily press. Colin Sheriff of Dunfermline bought a 6d Forth Road Bridge, which he spotted as a missing colour. With the firm intention of sending himself a first-day cover, he stuck it on and posted the envelope. Later it was sent to a large London auction house, and there realised £380. Another copy, this time mint, fetched exactly this figure at the same auction. A good return for a 6d outlay.

A sadder story was told by a businessman who bought some Post Office Savings Bank 2½ds and noted that the black colour was missing. He thought that they might have some curiosity value, and placing one in his wallet he gave the remainder to his secretary to file away. Two years later he was startled to read of the publicity and value given to the National Productivity Year Headless Queen. He sent for the file, only to discover that it had been cleared away and the contents destroyed. He looked into his wallet and found the one surviving example, rather rubbed, but quite presentable. He later sold it to a London dealer.

John Brian, a south London schoolboy, purchased a block of the International Telecommunications Union 1s 6d over the counter at the London Chief Office, after realising that the three he had already obtained for use on self-addressed first-day covers lacked the pink background. John's block came from the lower right hand corner with traffic lights. He explained later that he could only afford part of the complete sheet.

The greater the number of colours, the greater the chance that one will be missed in printing. Battle of Hastings 4d stamps were each printed in eight or nine colours. All except black are known to have been left out in turn, and one copy is known with both light blue and grey missing. Some of these are apparently fairly common and prices linger in the £15-£30

37. SPECIAL HANDSTAMPS
Handstamps are often sponsored by organisations. Most are in use
for only one day

38. ELIZABETHAN ERRORS

Top: Famous missing head of National Productivity Year issue (enlarged).

Centre: Partly imperforate. The perforating comb has missed one strike, leaving the top without separation on three sides.

Bottom: Parliamentary Conference missing gold colour. Post Office Tower missing colour, leaving one stamp without main motif

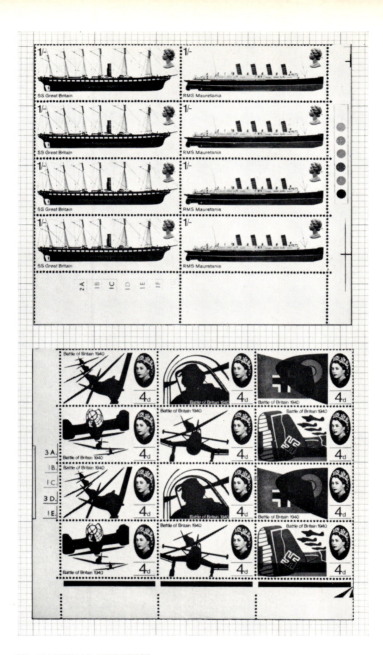

39. MARGINAL MARKINGS

Upper: Se-tenant ships with traffic lights in right margin, cylinder numbers in bottom gutter, and synchronisation marks partly visible at the right.

Lower: Battle of Britain cylinder numbers at left, and jubilee lines in the bottom gutter. Part of the marginal arrow also illustrated

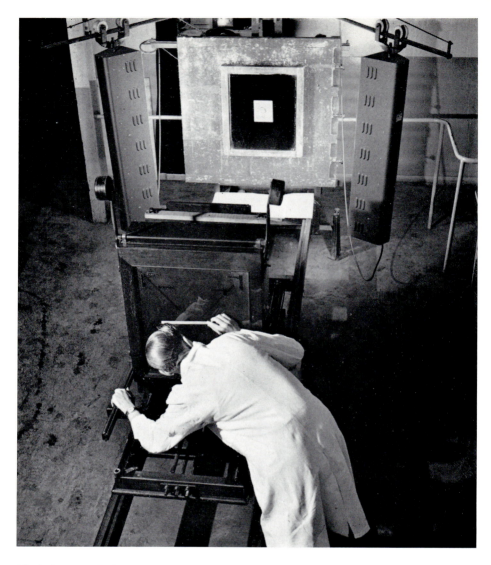

40. STAMP PRODUCTION—I
Preparing the camera to photograph the original drawing

range. Both denominations of the EFTA series, issued in February 1967, are known with missing colours. Most of the eight or nine colours involved affect only the row of flags, and certain colours are used only in a minute part of the design. Missing colours they may be, but so little do they affect the stamp that they can be worth less than five pounds.

Birds of 1966 was another set that seemed to run into colour difficulties. Unusual blocks of four with no feet, or other parts of the birds anatomy inexplicably missing were popular, and seven of the eight colours used disappeared one at a time. These stamps were printed through two machines, each printing four of the colours. One sheet is known to have by-passed one complete stage, and with four colours missing makes the record for a colour error in Great Britain.

Other errors are less spectacular, but just as full of philatelic interest. Watermarks inverted have a popular following, even though to the uninitiated all is well. The 9d Flower without watermark was being given away at one time by a dealer, as a free gift: at the other extreme, there are some so rarely met with that pounds are asked.

Similar in status are missing phosphor bands. Again almost invisible to a cursory glance, they are fairly common, fetching anything from a few pence to as many pounds. Perforation holes are made by a comb machine, which punches out a complete horizontal row and the vertical sides in that row, in one strike. If it fails, then there may be part perforated or imperforate errors. A fine example is found on the Jersey 2½d regional. The bottom row is known imperforate on three sides.

Perforation varieties are usually spotted and withdrawn, but it is harder to keep a check on complete booklets and there are a number of examples on record of partly imperforate panes. Each reported find brings forth the hopeful in their hordes with what they fondly imagine to be similar errors. Usually all they have are straight top, bottom or right side edges, the result of slightly inaccurate guillotining. Unhappily for the collector of perfect copies, straight edges are only too common. Imperforate stamps in booklets must have at least one gutter between stamps completely devoid of perforations. They are recorded for most issues, up to and including the present day, and fetch anything from £100 to £1000.

Another variety peculiar to booklets can occur when the paper somehow manages to get folded before separation. Stamps intended for an adjoining booklet remain unsevered, tucked inside the book. When folded out they form a combination known to collectors as tête-bêche, or head to tail. One stamp will be inverted with respect to the next. No British stamps have been issued this way by design. Until 1963, booklets were the only source of this type of variety, one or two a year finding their way into collections. Suddenly a large number of tête-bêche 3d stamps became available, and it was obvious that a sheet or more had leaked out onto the market. Copies were sold at from £5 to £10 a pair, despite warnings in the philatelic press that made it clear that they were stolen property. The epilogue came in December 1968, when among the possessions of Tony Mafia, a murdered gangster, were 700 tête-bêche 3d pairs. A press report outlined the find by the police at Brentwood, Essex. They noted that when the original supplies were on offer, Post Office investigators had established that the source originated among waste sheets of stamps. These had been stolen, instead of journeying to the incinerator.

One error gained prominence for a while. The Queen's cameo head in gold foil was missing from some specimens. This is rather a misnomer, for the foil contains no gold at all, but is a film coating of aluminium powder. The head is embossed from a specially treated Melinex polyster film of ICI Plastics. ICI supplied George M. Whitley Ltd, a long-established firm of gold leaf and thin metal manufacturers, with reels of 50 guage Melinex film. This was transformed into a hot stamping foil by the application of layers of coloured lacquers, and adhesive with the aluminium and the metal coating is deposited under vacuum. This treated film was then sent to the stamp printers, and the embossing brass, electrically heated, transferred the metallic foil under pressure onto the sheets of printed stamps. The metallic layer was released, the adhesive activated, binding the foil to the paper surface. It has been established that the foil can be removed, although most elementary methods leave some trace. Only expensive and sophisticated equipment can produce an almost undetectable 'missing head'. As this variety fetches only a moderate price, partly due to the widespread publicity of the forger's art, it has not been worthwhile to imitate it on a large scale.

Collectors tend to use the words variety and error indiscriminately. Error sounds more expensive than variety, so the word is overworked. A variety is any variation from the normally issued stamp. On recess-printed stamps the entry die may momentarily make contact in part, twice, and slight doubling of the design results. This is known as a re-entry. Later there may be attempts to touch up the plate to eliminate such extraneous lines, and the visible result is called a retouch. Such examples are interesting, but are not worth large sums. Damage may progressively get more noticeable as the printing proceeds, leaving some visible evidence to be found on the issued stamp. Later repairs or corrections to the printing cylinder or plate are also known as retouches.

Many small blemishes in modern photogravure stamps are considered unworthy of correction by the printers. There have from time to time been attempts by less reputable dealers to exploit collectors' gullibility by pretending that such spots and specks are of importance. They are almost invariably worth a small premium over the normal price for a stamp, but no more. Varieties are popular and will always be in demand. 'Flyspeck' philately is a term sneeringly used by the straightforward man, yet it can open the door to serious study and research.

Colour shifts must be considered to be a normal hazard of modern multicolour high-speed printing. If they measure but a millimetre or so, then no matter what the effect on the impression or design they remain minor varieties. They happen, they are common and are of little consequence. Major colour shifts are a different story. A corner block of four with cylinder markings of the first 9d Paintings issue, with figures of value so displaced that it was a full inch to the right, sold for £650 in auction, after a valuation of £450. But in this block one pair of stamps was without the Queen's head.

Perforation shifts are another common fault. In recent years the registration accuracy of the perforation holes has slackened. A perfect stamp requires perfect perforation with even margins all round the frame of the stamp. There has been an increasing tendency for this to be applied so far off true, that the holes cut into the picture of the design. Far from being worth more, they are valued at much less, not really deserving a place in a collection at all, for they are second-rate copies. Only when the holes approach the centre of the design does the collector again become interested. These are freaks, of curiosity value, fetching a few pounds per copy.

'Flyspecks' are only worth their place if they are constant, that is they occur on at least a substantial part of a printing. Then they will be entitled to at least a specialist catalogue mention. It always helps if the flaw gives the appearance of something tangible, such as an extra earring, or perhaps a lake in the middle of a map. Another worthwhile example occurred on the 1966 Christmas issue. The 'T' from the designers name T. Shemza was missing from the base of the stamp. Varieties that need a magnifying glass to be seen have strictly limited interest.

Only one variety of a transitory nature has been accorded universal recognition. This is the doctor blade flaw. For all recess methods, including photogravure, a doctor blade clears the face of the plate of surplus ink. Now and again the blade collects a minute piece of grit, leaving a trace of ink on the plate surface. This is printed, and when the lines are over a millimetre or so wide, they can be in demand.

Errors are the dream of a lifetime, and only the fortunate few will ever buy them over the counter. With a greater awareness of their importance, many clerks now check their stocks carefully. But familiarity can breed contempt, and there are still finds to be made on the definitive stamps. Varieties are possible for everyone and sheets of stamps are worth studying, if only as part of an observation exercise, before comparing results with those published in the philatelic press. Get varieties by all means, but recognise that there is little chance of capital appreciation. Once an issue is off sale, collectors are too busy with the newcomers to bother overmuch with those that went before.

15

Collecting Great Britain Elizabethans

Collecting stamps is a universal hobby. It knows no boundaries of class or age. Visit any post office on the first day of sale of the latest special set and there you will see some of the estimated million collectors in Great Britain alone. Few of them read a magazine, buy a catalogue or belong to a stamp club. The great unorganised, they hide away their new stamps, intending one day to mount them into an album or to hand them on to sons and daughters.

Stamps are relatively cheap, compared with other fields of collecting. Silver, paintings, porcelain, all require a hefty capital outlay to assemble even a small group. Stamps can cost a penny at the post office, rising to pounds for long off-sale specimens. Hundreds of pounds can be spent on early classic issues—over £100,000 was paid for one stamp in 1970 —but collectors of British Elizabethan stamps will rarely think of such amounts. It is possible, of course, to chase errors, but this is for the few. The many will be content with a representative selection, building on it as time allows. Errors are interesting, to be seen at exhibitions and in shop windows, but they are not an essential part of the hobby. Stamp collecting is what you make it. Fun, relaxation, the joy of completion, the pleasure in study, research, or just accumulating. It is all of this and more.

The true collector will be content with one copy of each stamp. When tempted, an extra one, or perhaps a block of four is put on one side as an investment. Investing in stamps, to make a profit, is possible, but it is not for the inexperienced.

Unless the stamps are bought at the post office, a dealer's margin is included in the selling price. This margin must be covered by appreciation in price, before any profit accrues at all. A few bad choices and the pleasing profit on one lot may be wiped out by the loss on another. Collectors of stamps, like any other art form, should if they choose wisely show a significant addition to their outlay, when the time comes to sell. But such profit is not the reason for collecting. The interest and contentment of many happy evenings, building up a country from hundreds of individual pieces is gain enough.

In the late 1960s, Great Britain stamps experienced a boom, the like of which had never been known in the country before. Advertisements appeared in the national as well as in the philatelic press. Dealers and companies sprung up like mushrooms. A new sort of advertisement appeared in the philatelic press with all the commemorative issues priced for both buyers and sellers, and special offers of complete sheets became commonplace. The age of speculation had arrived. Established collectors looked at the scene with sorrow and muttered uneasily of the damage it would cause to the hobby. They forecast that the bubble would burst with a vengeance.

The boom began when a few wideawake individuals realised that some of the early phosphor-lined stamps had very small printings, in many cases less than a million. They reasoned that most of these would have been used for postage, and stocks in collectors and dealers hands must be comparatively small. They advertised to buy them, and the cumulative force of these few buyers was enough to topple price stability. Almost overnight sets went up in price two- or three-fold, and then continued higher and higher. The boom was on.

As always, others jumped on the bandwagon. The man in the street, inexperienced, caught the whiff of money, and made a point of buying a complete sheet of every new issue. The press was full of reports of first-day queues and pictures of speculators buying hundreds of pounds of new stamps. In the confusion the prices continued to rise, and early buyers became sellers, at a profit, adding fuel to the flames. Suddenly speculation was at an end. Buying advertisements vanished, sellers' prices toppled in an effort to offload. Literally millions of stamps were available, for perhaps thousands of collectors. From twice the cost the burnt fingers of the speculator were lucky to get back 75 per cent of their outlay. British stamps were at a discount in the trade. The only really satisfied clients were the big business houses with a chance to cut down on their postage bills.

The bubble had burst, but the hobby did not really suffer. More new entrants than for many a day had come to realise that stamp collecting was a pleasing pursuit. They looked back at the commemorative chase, shrugged their shoulders, and started delving into definitives and earlier issues. Prices began to rise on all sides. Only the overspeculated commemoratives failed to make progress. Even the earlier phosphor commemoratives, that were the cause of all the fuss, held their price tag. New collectors were making some attempt at completion. In the due course of time, even today's spurned 'moderns' will recover as the excessive stocks are used up, and the ever-increasing true demand makes itself felt again.

One of the first decisions to be faced is the choice between mint and used. Probably the best answer to the uncommitted is to try and keep both going, until a definite preference is established. But even such a simple selection requires further consideration. Mint stamps, in philatelic parlance, are in the state that they were issued in. For years, such stamps were then placed in an album, by means of a hinge or mount. At the turn of the century, hinges were monstrous things, designed for their sticking power, but the miracles of modern technology have allowed more refined products to develop. Today a good-quality hinge is almost completely peelable, but there are few that do not leave some trace on the gum. Purists suggest that such stamps are no longer of top quality because they are not in Post Office condition. This movement, begun on the Continent, spread to Great Britain, and suddenly 'unmounted mint' was the vogue. It was carried to ridiculous extremes, with even the early classics sought after in such pristine freshness. Modern Great Britain Elizabethan stamps are all obtainable 'unmounted mint' but at a premium. So the choice remains— mounted or unmounted. Certainly unmounted stamps are in greater demand, and will probably continue to fetch higher selling prices.

Not that the collector of used stamps leads a simpler life. Look at the descriptions in common use: used, commercially used, good commercially used, good used, nice used, fine used, very fine used, and cancelled to order. That is one opinion of their ascending order of quality but opinions vary so much. There is little hope of standardisation from person to person. Cancelled to order stamps are those deliberately posted to receive a neat circular cancellation in the corner of the stamp. They may or may not have travelled through the posts. Very fine used are much the same quality. Always the aim is a neat light cancellation with some part of the postmark readable, not defacing the main sections of the design. It should not be smudged and the impression must not have disturbed the paper by indentation. Fine used are by definition just a little way off the top quality, unless they are bought from a dealer who wearies of too many descriptions. The whole world of descriptions is a confusing jungle. Aim for a stamp that looks fresh and clean, with a small postmark—a pleasure to add to the collection—and never mind the description!

It is so much easier to state the unacceptable. There can be no excuse for mounting stamps cancelled with wavy lines, or slogan portions. Parcel post killers, with their thick black lines, so deface a stamp as to make it look ugly. They may, if the cancellation has been lightly applied, fill a temporary gap, but they should be replaced as soon as possible. Smudged and unreadable postmarks are on the border line, a matter of taste. The best stamps will always fetch the highest prices when it is time to sell.

Commemoratives are the usual starting point for a serious collection, followed by the definitives. As has been seen, the first Queen Elizabeth permanent set is anything but straightforward, if the watermarks and phosphor lines are taken into account. Refuse to be put off by a succession of apparently identical pages. A true collector recognises that every unseen variation is part of the story. Prices of stamps are determined by supply and demand, and this short extract from a dealer's list underlines what can happen to a simple common stamp—the Wilding $2\frac{1}{2}$d on sale for 14 years.

Tudor watermark:
upright type 1 10p; type 2 20p; sideways 50p; inverted 25p.
St Edward watermark:

41. STAMP PRODUCTION—2
Retouching the negative before making the multipositive

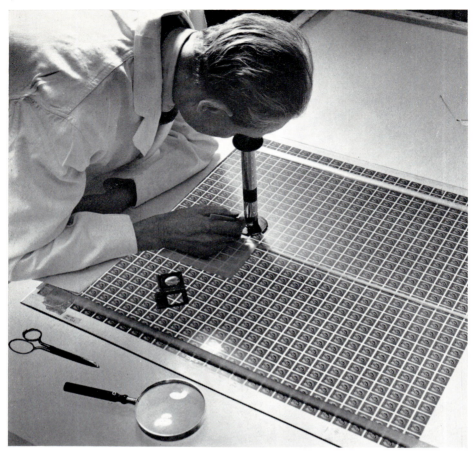

42. STAMP PRODUCTION—3
These large sheets are inspected, before making the multipositive.
This will contain a compact group of 480 (two post-office sheets)
impressions, from some part of this sheet

43. STAMP PRODUCTION—4
Preparations for the transfer of the multipositive to the carbon tissue

44. STAMP PRODUCTION—5
Those parts of the cylinder not required are painted out

45. STAMP PRODUCTION—6
Sometimes there are imperfections on the cylinder. Hand engraving
at this stage corrects such faults

46. STAMP PRODUCTION—7
The stamps come away from the printing unit in one long continuous
roll

47. STAMP PRODUCTION—8
Stamps are guillotined into double sheets of 480 prior to
perforation

48. STAMP PRODUCTION—9
The final check is one of the most important. They are examined for
flaws at high speed, by trained inspectors, to see that no imperfect
copies leave the printing works

upright type 1 10p; type 2 12p; sideways 20p; inverted 25p.
Graphite lines:
first watermark 40p; second watermark 75p; inverted £3.75;
phosphor £1.20.
Crown watermark:
upright type 1 12p; type 2 2p; chalky 10p; sideways type 1
8p; sideways type 2 20p; inverted 30p; chalky inverted 10p.
Phosphor lines only:
type 2, two bands 3p; type 2, one band 12p; type 1, one band
£1.50; inverted, two bands £11; inverted, one band £1.40.

Twenty-four stamps, apparently all identical to the untutored
eye, yet varying in their selling price from a couple of pence
to many pounds. They reach such high prices because there is
a genuine demand. It shows the wisdom of studying even the
commonest stamp.

The next step is more of a jump. Varieties are popular, but
there is the difficulty of nomenclature. Except for a few of the
freaks, varieties ought to be constant. Flaws in themselves are
interesting talking points; but if it can be shown, by following
a flaw through its life, that it at first develops, and later is
perhaps corrected, then a promising field of study may open up.

An alternative field for expansion is to leave the stamp and
go into the margins. The borders of Post Office sheets bristle
with one type of marking after another. Some are widely
collected, and a representative selection adds that little extra to
an otherwise straightforward display. First and foremost are the
cylinder and plate numbers. These usually appear in the left-
hand margin, opposite the 18th row of small-size definitives.
Collected in blocks of six, they include the bottom left-hand
corner of the sheet. They received a boost with the new Machin
Head stamps, and there are some attempts to collect every
different number. Some figures come with, and some without,
a dot, from two side by side cylinders, although they are always
separated into the conventional sheets before leaving the
printers. Perforation holes in the margins can add to the
number of possible varieties; they are characteristic of the
machine used. Modern high values carry a number, or number
and letter, in the lower right-hand margin. The earliest
printings of the Castle stamps do not show these particular

markings, and neither did the typographed postage due stamps. Many multicolour commemoratives have these numbers in non-standard positions.

Other markings are not so well known. Their study offers an insight into the methods of printing. Most multicolour printings are backed by check dots, now familiarly named traffic lights. These are solid circles, designed to give a quick visual check of the presence of each colour, and their alignment. Although one catalogue editor has stated that he does not consider them any more important than many other marginal markings, another one lists and prices them. There is room in the hobby for differences of opinion; these dots show in solid colour the actual basic tints used in the printing. Modern multicolour stamps blend and mix with subtlety; it is of interest to see the basic colours side by side.

The greatest problem facing printers with multicolour stamps is to see that the colours are synchronised, and that none are missing. Autotron marks, long bars, provide the electronic check for colour registration. Register marks, elongated crosses, one for each colour superimposed upon each other, serve a similar purpose. When all is well they present the impression of a single cross, but if slightly out they overlap. A small number of register crosses, in line touching each other, are used as a visual check. Some of these marks may be trimmed off, before the sheets reach the post office.

Thick coloured lines are frequently found under the bottom row of a sheet of photogravure stamps. They first appeared in the margins of British stamps in May 1887, the time of Queen Victoria's diamond jubilee, and they have been known as jubilee lines ever since. Their original purpose was to protect the printing plates against accidental damage. In those days, British stamps were printed by typography, and the printers' rule placed round the edge of the panes relieved the edges of the plates from the pressure which always falls more heavily on those parts.

Marginal arrows provide a visual indication to the counter clerk. They indicate the points of division into counter book panes, less unwieldy than complete sheets. Serial numbers are sometimes seen. Theoretically they provide a count on reel-fed printings, but they must not be taken seriously. Sheets are known with two different numbers when the counting mechanism has malfunctioned.

Recent sheets contain some indication of value. In the past, all sheets were issued with 240 small-size or 120 double-size stamps. There have been a number of departures from these standards, and this value indication (long used in some countries abroad) simplifies calculations.

Another new addition is a small number within a circle, applied by a rubber stamp. The Post Office explains that these are checkers marks. Batches of 1,000 sheets are broken down into 'lifts' of 25, and so these circles should appear on every twenty-fifth sheet.

Already the collector is departing from the straightforward printed listings. There are further unexplored avenues ahead. Postal stationery, semi-official and local carriage labels, postmarks and handstamps, all reflect personal taste, making a collection that little different from its thousands of fellows. But where to find this information, and how to house the result?

Most collectors will start with the listing in a catalogue. There are many to choose from, all with their faithful followers, as they appear, year by year.

One name is synonymous with stamp collecting: Stanley Gibbons Limited, dealers for many years, with their shop in the Strand, London, and their range of catalogues. A catalogue is basically a listing of stamps, with prices for both mint and used. There are a number of catalogues in the Gibbons range. *Stamps of the World*, which covers everything in one very large volume, ignoring watermarks, shades and perforations. The Big Gibbons, in many parts, with Great Britain in part one, the Commonwealth section. A more detailed listing of Great Britain is carried here, with some watermark varieties and shades, and all the details of perforations. Stanley Gibbons *Elizabethan Catalogue* carries far more detail, and as its name suggests, concerns itself only with Queen Elizabeth stamps. Varieties, more watermark variations, printing figures and details of issue are included.

Another widely used catalogue, the *Commonwealth Queen Elizabeth II Stamp Catalogue*, published by Urch Harris and Company Limited. This was the first of the specialised books of the reign, and it continues to contain many features unique to such a wide-ranging work.

To choose between them is a matter of taste. Stanley Gibbons *Elizabethan* contains magnified illustrations of all varieties, and its large-page format is clear and straightforward. All the stamps from one issue are listed in denomination order, with copious footnotes. The *Commonwealth* splits up the listings by type of watermark, and also includes booklet panes, and joined pairs from coils. Varieties roughly parallel the Stanley Gibbons list, but some are mentioned by only one of these books. The *Commonwealth* catalogue also prices cylinder blocks, traffic light blocks and first-day covers.

Prices are always a source of confusion. Stanley Gibbons catalogues are price lists, despite their use as works of reference. They state that quotations are their selling prices for stamps in fine condition, and reserve the right to change them. They do not guarantee to supply any particular stamp. The *Commonwealth* prices on the other hand are assessed on the basis of what is reasonable for a dealer to charge if asked for a specific stamp. They make the point that, if the dealer is somewhat overstocked with a particular item, he may be prepared to offer it at a lower price until his stock is balanced. Conversely, if he takes a lot of trouble to obtain a stamp for a customer, he could charge more.

Both catalogues are ideal starting points for a Great Britain collector of Queen Elizabeth stamps. They do, however, contain listings for the whole Commonwealth, so much of the contents may be unwanted. This is unavoidable, for the cost of any catalogue is a bargain in book-buying terms, made possible only by the number sold.

For a number of years there was only one specialised catalogue devoted solely to modern Great Britain stamps. *The Woodstock Catalogue of British Elizabethan Stamps* was first published in 1966, and each succeeding edition has improved what was in any case a major pioneering project. 260 pages cover the contents of this book in list form. Prices are culled from dealers' lists, auction realisations and a detailed knowledge of the market. Only mint stamps are priced individually, but used copies are quoted in sets.

Stanley Gibbons at last completed their *Great Britain Specialised Catalogue*, in August 1970. Volumes 1 and 2 had established themselves as serious works in the field, and the arrival of Volume 3, covering the Elizabethan issues, was greeted with interest. In this work the lists of the Wilding definitives are arranged value by value, and not by sets. This is particularly convenient in tracing the identity of a single stamp.

Woodstock and *Stanley Gibbons Specialised* are both daunting at first sight. *Woodstock* alone covers stationery and cinderella items, but some collectors prefer the Stanley Gibbons approach, and the knowledge that their prices are selling prices. A satisfactory solution, once the standard lists become too simplified, is to look at them both. Borrow them from your society or public library, and work with them.

Albums always present problems, and the final decision is so much one of personal taste. There are printed albums, with a space for every stamp, and in a few cases they are sold covering just the Elizabethan era. Even here there is a choice between a space, and a mounted strip which will take the specimen without mounting.

Loose-leaf blank albums exist in abundance. At an elementary level there are spring-back productions, in a range of sizes, and a variety of bindings. Slightly more expensive are the ring and peg-fitting groups which take the pages without bulging. and allow the pages to lie flat when the book is opened. Prices rise with the quality of the leaves (some of them are in fine card) and the sumptuousness of the binding. These albums carry purchase tax while illustrated ones escape. So some publishers carry a series with lightly printed stamps at the top of each leaf.

Interleaving should be considered essential, no matter which type of album is purchased. Stamps need to be protected against friction, and pressure. Only copies already safe behind strips, designed to hold stamps without touching the gum, have such protection.

Prices have been mentioned more than once. What is the correct value to place on a stamp? If it is still on free sale at the post office, then face value is enough. Once off sale the dealer is the most usual source of supply. A fair price then is one agreed between a willing buyer and a willing seller. No other value makes sense.

For run-of-the-mill items a rough average price is soon established. A walk around dealers' shops or stands at exhibitions will not disclose any startling variations. A look through the advertisements in any one of the many stamp periodicals will show the same picture. Prices do vary, and now and again perhaps alarmingly so. This is to be expected, for the dealer with the overheads of a shop and comprehensive stock cannot compete with the part-timer operating from home. Strangely, both may offer bargains in the long term. Any collector who intends to buy regularly cannot lose if he cultivates a dealer specialising in his particular interest.

A town-dweller may have a number of shops to choose from. In the small village, buying by post is the only answer to the perennial question—how to find a good source of supply. A reliable dealer is essential, one who is able to offer a range of wanted items. Cut-price offers are not so cheap when the postage both ways and cheque charges are added. Two or three reliable suppliers is a suitable goal—many will be content with only one.

Britain is served with a comprehensive philatelic press. Its pages are crammed with advertising, and after a few forays a trusted trader will emerge. In addition to stamps, he will probably be able to supply your albums and other accessories. In strict alphabetical order, the main magazines on general sale, and available by subscription or to special order are listed below.

Philatelic Bulletin, published by the Post Office, is a small pocket-sized monthly, with news about all forthcoming British stamps. It is particularly helpful for its feature portraying unaccepted designs, and for its reference articles on Post Office services. It is available only by subscription from the Philatelic Bureau.

Philatelic Magazine is an old-established independent, that carries supplements to the *Commonwealth* catalogue. Concentrating rather on the Commonwealth area, there are special Great Britain news pages. It is strong on Channel Islands news.

Stamp Collecting is a long-running independent weekly. The modern Great Britain collector will find it valuable for its up to the minute news from public and private sources. The Editor of the *Woodstock Catalogue* has a regular page, where he unravels puzzling facets of modern British stamps, and examines current issues.

Stamp Magazine is another independent, part of the Link House group. It attracts more advertising than any other magazine, and is often bought for that alone. It prints supplements to the *Elizabethan* catalogue, and there are a number of popular features, including a varieties page which always draws a full mail bag. Modern Great Britain developments are not overlooked.

Stamp Monthly is the house journal of Stanley Gibbons Limited. In addition to general articles it contains news items and complete supplements to all the firm's catalogues. It is fully illustrated, with the accent on information and entertainment.

Stamp Weekly, the youngster of the group, is a newspaper, making full use of its modern printing process to include colour and up-to-date news. Every new Great Britain stamp appears on the front cover in full colour, and there is hardly a week without a racy, but informative piece, on some aspect of Great Britain collecting.

Which is the one for you? The only sensible advice is to look at them all, choose two or three for a trial run, before settling down to your favourites.

It is strange that so many collectors curl themselves up with their stamps and never meet another enthusiast. There has been a concerted effort throughout the country to start stamp clubs, and very successful they are. They exist in towns and villages, suburbs and factories, offices and schools. Once convinced, members attend regularly, gaining from the knowledge of others and offering their own in exchange. They are sociable meetings, but you must take the first step. Your local library will be able to supply the name and address of the Secretary of the club nearest to you, or a letter to any magazine editor would do as well. If by chance there is no club nearby, then how about calling a meeting through your local press and starting one yourself?

In addition to the local societies there are a number of national organisations.

The National Philatelic Society, with its headquarters at 44 Fleet Street, London E.C.4, welcomes into membership anyone interested in stamps. It offers a bi-monthly magazine, comfortable London headquarters, and a library with a strong Great Britain section. 'Exchange packets' circulate, and there is a Great Britain section. 'Exchange packets' are no longer an exchange medium as such, although that is their historical origin. Now they are boxes of say 20 books, sent in by members, filled with their duplicates, all clearly priced. Take those you want, send the money to the organiser, and post the box onto the next address on the list. This circulating method enables stamps to be seen by 20-30 collectors, and each in turn just pays one lot of postage, in addition to purchases.

Foremost in Great Britain is the Royal Philatelic Society, 41 Devonshire Place, London w.1. It is not cheap, but it offers much. A complete library, meetings in luxurious surroundings, it is by no means exclusive. Every amateur is welcomed, but anyone dealing in stamps is ineligible for membership.

The specialist should consider the Great Britain Philatelic Society, for it offers many features unobtainable elsewhere. Its newsletters and magazines contain much information too detailed to appear in the commercial philatelic press. All members share the common interest of Great Britain, and due to the vastness of the field, there are sections for different periods and themes. There is one for the Queen Elizabeth stamps only. This is the society to find straightforward collectors according to Stanley Gibbons catalogues, and specialists in the byeways from stationery to locals. Meetings are held in London throughout the year.

Collect, study and research your stamps. Share your findings with others and pick their brains. Read all you can, not only in the catalogues, but also articles and books that cover your interest. Write to magazines, with queries and ideas. Join the local club and a national one too. Enjoy the hobby to the full. Stamp collecting may be as sedentary or as active as you choose. For you, and for the million others like you.

Appendix One

Periodicals and Publications

PERIODICALS

Aero Field, Francis J. Field, Sutton Coldfield, Warwickshire.
London Philatelist, Royal Philatelic Society, London, 41 Devon-
shire Place, London W1N 1PE
Philatelic Bulletin, 2-4 Waterloo Place, Edinburgh, EH1 1AB
Philatelic Journal of Great Britain, 50 Pall Mall, London SW1
Philatelic Magazine, 42 Maiden Lane, London WC2N 6HQ
The Philatelist, 50 Pall Mall, London SW1
Philately, British Philatelic Association, 446 Strand, London
WC2
Railway Philately, Railway Philatelic Group, 59a Hartley Road,
Kirkby-in-Ashfield, Nottingham NG17 8DS
Stamp Collecting, 42 Maiden Lane, London WC2N 6HQ
Stamp Lover, National Philatelic Society, 44 Fleet Street, Lon-
don EC4
Stamp Magazine, Link House, Dingwall Avenue, Croydon CR9
2TA
Stamp Monthly, 391 Strand, London WC2
Stamp Weekly, Link House, Dingwall Avenue, Croydon CR9
2TA

BOOKS

Some of the volumes listed may be out of print, but most are
available on loan to members of the National Philatelic Society,
and the Royal Philatelic Society, London, through their respective libraries. Public libraries may also be able to obtain them

through the national lending scheme.

Postal Arrangements to cover the issue of Commemorative Postage Stamps of the UK, Langston and Wellsted

The Complete List of Flaws on Queen Elizabeth Great Britain 1st Design Stamps for Booklets and Coils, C. Langston

Slogan Postmarks of the United Kingdom and supplements, C. R. H. Parsons and G. R. Pearson

Current Machine Postmarks of the UK, B. Bennett

Commemorative Postage Stamps of Great Britain, L. N. and M. Williams

Great Britain Airway Letter Stamps and Services, N. C. Baldwin

Talyllyn Railway Letter Stamps and Postal History, D. Potter

CATALOGUES

Stanley Gibbons Priced Postage Stamp Catalogue—British Commonwealth

Stanley Gibbons Elizabethan Stamp Catalogue

Commonwealth Queen Elizabeth Stamp Catalogue

The Woodstock Catalogue of British Elizabethan Stamps

Stanley Gibbons Great Britain Specialised Catalogue—Volume 3—Queen Elizabeth

Specialised Catalogue of Channel Islands Stamps, Channel Islands Specialist Society (33 Halfway Street, Sidcup, Kent)

Catalogue of Great Britain Railway Letter Stamps—1957 On, Railway Philatelic Group (18 Queens Road, Hale, Altrincham, Cheshire)

Appendix Two

Principal Postage Rates—Inland

LETTER POST

1 May 1952	2 ounces 2½d, 4 ounces 3d, then 1d for each additional 2 ounces
1 January 1956	2 ounces 2½d, then 1½d for each additional 2 ounces
1 October 1957	1 ounce 3d, 2 ounces 4½d, then 1½d for each additional 2 ounces
17 May 1965	2 ounces 4d, each additional 2 ounces up to 1 pound 2d, each additional 2 ounces 3d
3 October 1966	2 ounces 4d, each additional 2 ounces up to 1 pound 2d, each additional 2 ounces up to 1½ pounds 3d, 1½ to 2 pounds 3s 6d, each additional 1 pound 2s

POSTCARDS

1 May 1940	2d
1 October 1957	2½d
17 May 1965	3d

PRINTED MATTER

1 June 1951	4 ounces 1½d, each additional 2 ounces ½d
1 January 1956	2 ounces 1½d, each additional 2 ounces 1d
1 June 1956	4 ounces 2d, each additional 2 ounces 1d
1 October 1957	2 ounces 2d, 4 ounces 4d, each additional 2 ounces 1d

1 October 1961   2 ounces 2½d, 4 ounces 4d, each additional
                   2 ounces 1d
17 May 1965   2 ounces 3d, 4 ounces 5d, each additional
                   2 ounces 1d

TWO-TIER POSTAGE

The different postage rates for various types of mail were abandoned, and a two-tier system introduced, offering a choice of service, first-class or second-class.
16 September 1968

First Class
4 ounces 5d, 6 ounces 9d, each additional 2 ounces to 1½ pounds
3d, 2 pounds 4s, each additional pound 2s

Second class
4 ounces 4d, each additional 2 ounces to 18 ounces 2d, each additional 2 ounces to 1½ pounds 1d, maximum 1½ pounds

REGISTRATION

1 May 1952   6d, limit of compensation £5
1 June 1956   1s, limit of compensation £10
1 February 1961   1s 6d, limit of compensation £20
29 April 1963   1s 9d, limit of compensation £20
3 October 1966   3s, limit of compensation £100

There were facilities, for higher compensation cover, at additional fees.

SHILLINGS/PENCE—DECIMAL CONVERSION

These conversion rates are those supplied by the Decimal Currency Board. There are no exact conversion factors for small amounts, and it is in this area that most postage rates lie. In addition the ½d was withdrawn in 1969, prior to Great Britain going decimal.

2½p=6d, 5p=1s and so on in proportion, exactly
½p=1d, 1p=2d or 3d, 1½p=4d, 2p=5d, 3p=7d, 3½p=8d,
4p=9d or 10d, 4½p=11d; these are only approximate equivalents.

INDEX

Index